HULLABALOO!

WEST COUNTRY

Edited by Lynsey Hawkins

First published in Great Britain in 2003 by
YOUNG WRITERS
Remus House,
Coltsfoot Drive,
Peterborough, PE2 9JX
Telephone (01733) 890066

All Rights Reserved

Copyright Contributors 2003

SB ISBN 1 84460 226 5

FOREWORD

Young Writers was established in 1991 as a foundation for promoting the reading and writing of poetry amongst children and young adults. Today it continues this quest and proceeds to nurture and guide the writing talents of today's youth.

From this year's competition Young Writers is proud to present a showcase of the best poetic talent from across the UK. Each hand-picked poem has been carefully chosen from over 66,000 'Hullabaloo!' entries to be published in this, our eleventh primary school series.

This year in particular we have been wholeheartedly impressed with the quality of entries received. The thought, effort, imagination and hard work put into each poem impressed us all and once again the task of editing was a difficult but enjoyable experience.

We hope you are as pleased as we are with the final selection and that you and your family will continue to be entertained with *Hullabaloo! West Country* for many years to come.

CONTENTS

Abbas & Templecombe CE Primary School, Templecombe
William Foers	1
Daniel Moore	1
Stephen Flagg	2
Ben Ballard	2
Adam Burt	3
Ashlie Brabon	3
Matthew Biddiscombe	4
Sam Moorse	4
Emily Sherry	5
Tiffany Fudge	5
Melissa Pitman	6
Ellie Moore	6
Samantha Parker	7
David Symonds	7
Sam Benjafield	8
Jason Phillips	9

Ashcombe Primary School, Weston-super-Mare
Jake Moss Bezzina	9
Christina Milsom	10
Dylan Kone	10
Bridie Middlemiss	10
Christian Nelson	11
Dale Carter	11
Stephanie Jones	11
Lily Goodwin	12
Jade Waplington	12
Sam Webb-Wood	13
Rebecca McInally	13
Daniel Gardner	14
Katie Hyde	14
Louise Chubb	15
Deanna Kay Harper	15
Simone Suzanne Leigh-Willmore	16
Amy Elizabeth Kettle	16

Danielle Quick	16
Nathan Brand	17
Jade Shearer	17
Stellios Lee Koustounis	17
Jasmin Hillman	18
Lauren Davis	18
Ben Corcoran	19
Billie Davies	19
Holly Tucker	20
Oliver Wilkins	20
Yasmin La Touche	21
Portia Coburn	21
Ryan Tomkins	22
Joshua Farrow	22
Chloe Davies	22
Evie Redford	23
Lucy Keedwell	23
Thomas Sage	24
Tamsin Macbeath	24
Micah-Josie Denmead	25
Mollie Neal	25
Laura Escott	25
Becky Light	26
Emily Tyrrell	26
Oliver Loud	27
Sarah Knott	27
Kelsie-Rose Edwards	28
Emily Sims	29
Philip Howe	30
Elliott Green	30
Charley Hearne	31

Freshford VC Primary School, Bath

Lauren Brimble	31
Lauren Hockenhull	32
Milly Palastre	32
Lily Moffatt	32
Rossana Padget	33

Emily Tucker	34
Alice Horler	34

Kewstoke Primary School, Weston-super-Mare

Christopher Jones & Michael Deane	35
Sophie Jones & Emily Davies	36
Jennifer Tate & Kayleigh Harris	37
Thomas Heeney	38

North Petherton Junior School, Bridgwater

Paige Copsey & Rebecca Smart	38
Jevon Wheeler, Ben Woodrow & James Fox	39
Lee Llewellyn & Joe Ellis	39
Philip Prince, Daniel Pike & Patrick McCarthy	39
Robert Sturgeon	40
Kathleen Bullock & Hayley Duddridge	41
Laura Flaherty	41

Norton Fitzwarren CE VC Community School, Taunton

Jacob Gamble	42
Ben Jewell	42
Jessie Smith	42
Lee Phillips	43
Olivia Baggley	43
Ryan Hallett	44
Josh Williams	44
Josh Summers	44
Leanne Robertson	45
Christopher Manuel	45
Jordan Hawkins	46
Terri Joyner	46
Jessica Sillett	46
Kristopher Speechly	47
Olivia Pring	47
Jessica Cornish	48
Daniel Cooke	48

Kirsty Mabley	49
Charlotte Callun	49
Tiffany Rustage	50
Amy Bond	50
Jade Groody	50
Rhys Sykes	51
Naomi Williams	51
Josh Mattravers	52
Gemma Dalton	52

Oldfield Park Junior School, Bath

Ross Ashman	53
Rebecca Wall	53
James Butt	54
Andrew Bean	54
Holly Lakeman	55
Oliver Ashley-Owen	55
Scott Jardine	56
Laurence Kemp	56
Damien Evered	56
Chevenell McRae	57
Jessica Asquith-Dagger	57
Sam Light	57
Natasha Harris	58
Josh Southard Williams	58
Hannah Woodland	59
Olivia Dellow	59
Gemma Eades	60
Adele Wallis-Poulton	60
Holly Aldous	60
Nathan Gormley	61
Daniel Ashworth	61
Gemma Broad	62
Florence Hinton-Collyer	62
Catherine Bradbeer	63
Josh Catchpool	63
Callum Ball	64
Kyle Norris	64

David Locke	65
Craig Wall	65
Lauren Blackmore	66
Amy North	67
Laurence Murray	68
William Robinson	68
Jessica Archer	69
Sam Meopham	69
Benjamin Laslett	69
Emma Walker	70
Peter Sixsmith	70
Morwenna Harrington	71
Jessica Ball	71
Georgia Sheppard	72
Aaron Farnham	72
Serena Wall	73
Kieran Cox	73
Iqubal Hussain	74
Seb Burvill	74
Claire Kingwell	75
Rachel Eades	75
Matthew Arthurs	76
Thomas Fry	76
Samuel Melbourne	77
Sophie Burman	77
Jessica Newman	78
Emily Whittock	78
Sam Hughes	79
Emma Miller	79
Jessica Banks	79
Abigail Strange	80
Jordan Short	80
Tom Lakeman & Michael Cook	80
Zoë Macey	81
Daniel Renwick	81
Jacob Ives	82
Charleigh Fry	82
Emily Tolley	83

Jasmine White	83
Philip Durham	84
Chelsea Buchan	84
Verity Bean	85
Charlotte Lakeman	85
Katie Minchin	86
Stacey Jones	87

St Benedict's RC Primary School, Midsomer Norton

Nervana Barron	87
Marie-Louise Kertzman	88
Benedict Harrington	88
Laura Kor	89
Catherine Singh	89
Lara Cockhill	89
Robert Spence	90
Jessica Winsley & Flora Stevens	90
Sophie Symons	91
Harry Morris	91
Jennifer Liddle	92
Amy Milverton	92
Matthew Mitchell	92
Anna Moon	93
Lucy Francis	93
Katherine Fox	94
Charlotte Jones	94
Tom Gould	94
Sam Weller	95
Bryony McDermott	95

St Julian's Primary School, Bath

Joseph Segal	95
Hannah Langley	96
William Hughes	96
Zoe Robertson	97
Jade Dix	97
Oliver McGill	97

Wiveliscombe Primary School, Taunton

Sam Vercoe	98
Rosie Johnson	98
Sophie Prescott	99
Freddie Kimsey	99
Jessica Robinson	100
Andrew Fudge	100
Andrew Heard	101
Charley Chandler	102
Alfie Callery	102
Ruby-Ann Boddington Parker	103
Ben Toomer	103
Eleanor Finlayson	104
James Adams	104
Rachael Bashford	105
Max Norman	105
Rhianna White	106
Catherine Shackleton	107
Georgia McGovern	107

Yeo Moor Junior School, Clevedon

Jamie Ellis	108
Pagan Knill	108
Lauren Burman	109
Sam Ford	109
Becky Hilder	110
Sarah Gazzard	110
Alex Corrigan	111
Ashley Thornton	111
Andrew Ham	112
Josh Cope	112
Aaron Bray	113
Philippa Crossland	113
Freja Lovett	114
Sam Kacher	115
Ashley Williams	116
Helen Newell	116
Jessica Puddy	117

Evey Carpenter	117
Zara Thomas	118
Emily Ayres	118
Jack Courtney	119
Rhianne Williams	119

The Poems

I LOVE PETS

I love pets,
I've go loads.
But my favourite are
Frogs and toads.

I've got iguanas,
They love to eat bananas
And all my monkeys
Love to climb trees.

I also love dogs,
But they like chasing hogs
And as for my cats
All they will eat is rats.

I love pets,
It's clear to see,
So I've got my own
Animal sanctuary!

William Foers (11)
Abbas & Templecombe CE Primary School, Templecombe

DOLPHINS

D olphins swim with hardly any effort,
O r they go underwater and catch fish.
L ove the beautiful dolphins,
P lay with them all day.
H ave fun with the dolphins
I n the water and above.
N or will they bite you,
S wim with them as long as you like.

Daniel Moore (9)
Abbas & Templecombe CE Primary School, Templecombe

SPACE ALIEN

There was a small spaceship
an alien inside,
pressing all the buttons
for a nasty ride.

It had sixteen arms and it had two heads
waving all around,
as well, it had five legs and five feet
all jumping off the ground.

It was crashing and bashing
turning up and down,
it was chucking and throwing things
I had a frown.

Soon the alien stopped
and waved goodbye,
it got into its spaceship
and started to fly.

Stephen Flagg (9)
Abbas & Templecombe CE Primary School, Templecombe

MY PET COLLIE . . .

Is big, black and white,
His ears flop over and has a spotty nose.
He has big blue eyes and a hard head,
He loves to run and play and he sleeps in my room.
I love him loads and loads
And he makes me really happy when I am sad.

Ben Ballard (10)
Abbas & Templecombe CE Primary School, Templecombe

MY NEW DOG

M y new dog will be a loyal and brave dog.
Y oung people like me love dogs.

N ice my old dog was, a golden Labrador.
E xcitement, that was all I felt when I heard about
W oof, that is my new dog's name.

D umb he was at first, he would hit walls.
O h what a laugh we had with Woof.
G od took him away when he was only twelve.

Adam Burt (10)
Abbas & Templecombe CE Primary School, Templecombe

MUSIC WORRY

I'm sitting on my stall,
Bow in my hand.
I'm so nervous,
No one understands.

There's a cello by my side
As I begin to play.
Am I going to get it wrong,
Can't we do this another day?

The notes are squiggling on the page.
When is it going to be over?
Good job I've got a lucky charm,
Which is a four-leaved clover.

Ashlie Brabon (11)
Abbas & Templecombe CE Primary School, Templecombe

MY PETS

My cat is Pickles, who is black and white,
He doesn't go out at night,
But he get in loads of fights.
He goes out hunting for birds and mice,
He thinks they taste very nice.

My dog is Bracken, who is black and brown,
He loves to smile and hates to frown.
He likes to play with his teddy
And loves a bit of roast and gravy.

Bracken and Pickles play all day,
They love to play and play and play.
They are always very nice,
But sometimes like to play fight.

Matthew Biddiscombe (11)
Abbas & Templecombe CE Primary School, Templecombe

ME AND YOU

Me and you are different!
I have blue eyes, you have pink!
I have blond hair you have green!
I have normal lips, yours are bright red!
I have a normal nose, you have two noses!
I have four fingers and a thumb, you have ten fingers and five thumbs!
I have five toes, you have ten toes!
Can you guess who's my friend?

He's an alien!

Sam Moorse (10)
Abbas & Templecombe CE Primary School, Templecombe

GRANDAD

My grandad is a funny man,
He likes to mess about.
He likes to tell us funny jokes,
Which makes us laugh and shout.

My grandad visits most Friday nights,
He brings my nanny too!
In the morning he sings us songs,
His favourite's about Lulu.

I love my grandad lots and lots,
My brother does as well.
He's a very kind and thoughtful man,
Sixty or seventy? Who can tell!

Emily Sherry (8)
Abbas & Templecombe CE Primary School, Templecombe

THE DEVIL AT SCHOOL

The Devil is among us,
He could be riding the school bus.

The Devil is among us,
He could be getting an A+.

The Devil is among us,
Using our school brush.
I don't know if it's true,
But I think the Devil might be *you!*

Tiffany Fudge (10)
Abbas & Templecombe CE Primary School, Templecombe

MY BEDROOM

My bedroom's always tidy,
It's never in a mess.
My bedroom is always cleaned on a Friday,
But now it needs it less.

My bedroom's full of colours,
I couldn't dream of it being dull,
Everybody thinks it's too much,
But I think it's cool.

My mum says, 'Come on or else you'll be late!'
But I'm too busy sleeping in my nice warm bed.
My bedroom is as big as a hall,
'It's too big!' my mum has always said.

My room is always top of the class,
It's mine and I like it.
But I won't let anyone say that
Mine's the best in the world!

Melissa Pitman (10)
Abbas & Templecombe CE Primary School, Templecombe

MY PONY

My pony is called Marmaduke, he is 28 years old.
He lives in a rug, it keeps him snug
And stops him getting cold.
He liks his hacks and snacks.

My pony Marmaduke has a best friend called Tom,
They like to play together in the sun.
He licks his bucket until the food has gone!

Ellie Moore (8)
Abbas & Templecombe CE Primary School, Templecombe

SPACE AND PLANETS

S tars surround Mars!
P eople investigate!
A stronauts on the moon!
C ircles for planets!
E arth spinning around!

A dventures around!
N ever go to the sun!
D isasters with rockets!

P eople get excited!
L asting all day!
A tmosphere is light!
N aughty children trash things!
E veryone screams!
T ake-off is ready!
S unny everywhere!

Samantha Parker (10)
Abbas & Templecombe CE Primary School, Templecombe

ELEPHANTS

E lephants make such
L ovely companions
E lephants
P rancing over canyons,
H appy and joyful
A nd never a care
N ice - just
T o be hunted,
S o unfair!

David Symonds (11)
Abbas & Templecombe CE Primary School, Templecombe

Sunshine All The Time, Any Day

S unshine sometimes,
U mbrellas if needed,
N ever to rain again,
S hining all day long,
H eat all the time.
I n and out of the sun,
N ormally it is hot,
E veryone is having *fun*

A lways fun all the time,
L ying under the sun,
L iving near the sun.

T hese people like the sun,
H aving to put on suntan lotion,
E veryone is enjoying it.

T all people, short people,
I gloos are ready for them to cool down in.
M aking everyone sweat
E Each day, getting hotter.

A sking for an ice cream,
N obody will miss the sun
Y achts in the deep blue sea.

D ying for a glass of water
A nyone can see
Y ou like the sun.

Sam Benjafield (11)
Abbas & Templecombe CE Primary School, Templecombe

IF . . .

If all the seas were one sea,
what a great sea that would be.
If all the trees were one tree,
what a great tree that would be.
If all the axes were one axe,
what a great axe that would be.
If all the men were one man,
what a great man that would be
and if that great man took the great axe
and cut down the great tree
and let it fall into the great sea
what a *splish-splash* that would be!

Jason Phillips (9)
Abbas & Templecombe CE Primary School, Templecombe

RAINBOW

Rain and sun make a beautiful sight,
In the sky,
When I see the colours,
My heart gleams like a star,
The rain falls slowly down
And I let it drip on me,
It's like magic,
I feel so happy,
Every time it glows,
The rainbow's gone,
But there might be one tomorrow.

Jake Moss Bezzina (7)
Ashcombe Primary School, Weston-super-Mare

Rainbow

R ainbow, rainbow shining bright
A s the rainbow shines towards the sun
I n the sky when the rainbow's shining by the sea
N ow the rainbow's made
B lue and red and yellow and violet
O ver the rivers and the houses
W here the rainbow fades away.

Christina Milsom (7)
Ashcombe Primary School, Weston-super-Mare

Rainbow

R ainbow, rainbow shines bright
A mber, red and green over houses
I nky-blue and sweet pink
N ow the colours mix
B ye-bye I say when they fade away
O ver the moon and stars
W hen it goes away.

Dylan Kone (7)
Ashcombe Primary School, Weston-super-Mare

Rainbow Rainbow

R ainbow, rainbow,
A ll the colours of the world
I n strips and runs
N ow it looks like magic
B eginning to blow away
O ver the houses
W orking to fade away.

Bridie Middlemiss (7)
Ashcombe Primary School, Weston-super-Mare

RAINBOW

R ain and sun together make the sky bright
A ll the colours in the rainbow sparkle like the sun
I n the rainbow the colours bloom like flowers
N ow the coloured ribbons are lighting up the sky
B ig rainbows in the sky
O range, yellow, pink and blue
W hen the rainbow fades away I wish it could stay.

Christian Nelson (8)
Ashcombe Primary School, Weston-super-Mare

RAINBOW

R ed, orange, green, blue
A ll colours together
I n the rainbow
N ow I feel happy and
B low the colours away
O ver the hills and far away
W here do they keep the rainbow?

Dale Carter (8)
Ashcombe Primary School, Weston-super-Mare

BONFIRE NIGHT

Rockets are whooshing really high,
Fountains brighten up the sky.
Catherine wheels spin really fast,
Bonfire Night's such a blast!

Stephanie Jones (7)
Ashcombe Primary School, Weston-super-Mare

BONFIRE NIGHT

Tonight's the night for the fireworks,
To blast-off into the sky,
Children are watching the fireworks,
Whizzing up really high,
Now is the time for the food to be eaten,
Until there's no food on the plate,
My mum says I can go and play
With my best mate,
Now is the time for the fireworks,
To blast-off into the night,
When they're halfway up,
They explode with flashes of light,
Now is the time to go home,
With my aching head,
All the fireworks are done for the night,
I'll snuggle into bed.

Lily Goodwin (8)
Ashcombe Primary School, Weston-super-Mare

RAINBOW POEM

Red and green and yellow and blue
Shines so bright all silvery-white.

It is shining and exciting
It sparkles in my eye.

Now we see it,
Now we don't
Beautiful rainbow.

Jade Waplington (7)
Ashcombe Primary School, Weston-super-Mare

EVENING

Evening comes
  With children playing noisily

Evening comes
  With PlayStations whirling.

Evening comes
  With children playing rugby noisily.

Evening comes
  With dinners cooking deliciously.

Evening comes
  With sky darkening slowly.

Evening comes
  With the TV flashing brightly.

Evening comes!

Sam Webb-Wood (9)
Ashcombe Primary School, Weston-super-Mare

RAINBOW

R ed yellow green and blue
A s they mix together
I n the sky
N ow the rainbow shines bright
B ut the rainbow goes away
O ver the hills
W hen the rainbow goes away
  I say, 'Goodbye come again!'

Rebecca McInally (7)
Ashcombe Primary School, Weston-super-Mare

WINTER

Winter comes
>with snow falling slowly.

Winter comes
>with paths freezing quickly.

Winter comes
>with snowmen sinking steadily.

Winter comes
>with stars shining brightly.

Winter comes
>with children playing cheerfully.

Winter comes
>with people chatting loudly.

Winter comes
>with fires burning beautifully.

Daniel Gardner (8)
Ashcombe Primary School, Weston-super-Mare

RAINBOW

R ainbow, rainbow in the sky
A re you happy?
I n the sky
N ow all the colours fade
B lue
O range
W here do they go?

Katie Hyde (7)
Ashcombe Primary School, Weston-super-Mare

EVENING

Evening comes
  With fires burning brightly
Evening comes
  With children watching TV quietly
Evening comes
  With children eating noisily
Evening comes
  With windows shutting quickly
Evening comes
  With curtains closing slowly
Evening comes
  With children sleeping peacefully
Evening comes
  With people snoring loudly
Evening comes
  With toys packing silently
Evening comes.

Louise Chubb (9)
Ashcombe Primary School, Weston-super-Mare

RAINBOW SHINING BRIGHT

R ed and violet, green and orange
A re all the colours of the rainbow
I n the sky
N ow the rainbow is beautiful in the distance.
B right and fabulous
O ver houses and homes
W hen suddenly it fades away.

Deanna Kay Harper (8)
Ashcombe Primary School, Weston-super-Mare

Rainbow

R ed, yellow, green and blue
A ll together and
I like a lovely rainbow
N ow I can watch the rainbow fades away
B ouncing off to go and play
O n the seaside I
W atch it play and suddenly it's time to fade away . . .

Simone Suzanne Leigh-Willmore (8)
Ashcombe Primary School, Weston-super-Mare

Rainbow

R ed, yellow, pink and blue
A re part of a rainbow just for you
I ndigo, violet
N ext comes blue, feel the
B reeze
O ver you
W hen the rainbow fades away we will have a happy day.

Amy Elizabeth Kettle (7)
Ashcombe Primary School, Weston-super-Mare

Rainbow

R ed is pretty, so is orange
A ll the colours in the rainbow
I t is shining and exciting
N ow we see, now you don't
B eautiful colours, beautiful rainbow
O ver the houses, over the fields
W hen it's there it fades away.

Danielle Quick (8)
Ashcombe Primary School, Weston-super-Mare

RAINBOW

R ainbow, rainbow
A ll the colours shining bold
I n the sky, over fields
N ow the rainbow's done
B lue and orange
O ver the towns
W hen I see it I feel lucky!

Nathan Brand (8)
Ashcombe Primary School, Weston-super-Mare

BONFIRE NIGHT

Whooshing fireworks exploding in the night sky.
Rockets going so high up into the sky.
Catherine wheels spinning on the gate at night.
Sparklers sparkling in the dark.
Sausages burning on fires outside.
Children eating soup.
It's Bonfire Night.

Jade Shearer (7)
Ashcombe Primary School, Weston-super-Mare

BONFIRE NIGHT

Rockets exploding in the air - *bang, boom!*
Catherine wheels spinning,
Children and adults eating chips
And sausages burning on the fire.
Lovely colours flying in the sky,
What a fantastic night it is.

Stellios Lee Koustounis (8)
Ashcombe Primary School, Weston-super-Mare

WINTER COMES

Winter comes
With lightning flashing
Winter comes
With puddles splashing
Winter comes
With rain pouring
Winter comes
With snowman laughing
Winter comes
With people sneezing
Winter comes with
People playing
Winter ends
With spring coming.

Jasmin Hillman (8)
Ashcombe Primary School, Weston-super-Mare

BONFIRE NIGHT

Remember, remember the 5th of November,
When the Catherine wheels spin.
Rockets bang up in the sky.
Children screaming, getting excited.
Sausages sizzling,
Spitting,
Fizzing all night,
What a fantastic bright night!

Lauren Davis (7)
Ashcombe Primary School, Weston-super-Mare

BONFIRE NIGHT

November 5th is Bonfire Night,
Catherine wheels are lovely,
When they spin,
Zooming rockets
Exploding in the air,
Making a beautiful scene,
I love the smell of sausages and chips,
Fountains lighten up the sky,
Like a big fire,
Bonfire Night is when children
Make funny faces with glittering sparklers,
Now we have to go home,
It was a great time,
I love Bonfire Night.

Ben Corcoran (7)
Ashcombe Primary School, Weston-super-Mare

BONFIRE NIGHT

Sparklers are sparkling
Burgers are burning
Catherine wheels are spinning
Boom!
Blast!
Zoom!
Whizz!
Fireworks are popping
Rockets are crashing
Sausages are sizzling!

Billie Davies (7)
Ashcombe Primary School, Weston-super-Mare

WINTER COMES

Winter comes
With red robins singing
Winter comes
With wind howling
Winter comes
With snowflakes falling
Winter comes
With thunder roaring
Winter comes
With lightning flashing
Winter comes
With a breeze whistling
Winter comes
With the sea rising
Winter ends
With sunny bright spring!

Holly Tucker (9)
Ashcombe Primary School, Weston-super-Mare

BONFIRE NIGHT

Fireworks zoom up and down slowly,
Catherine wheels spin round
As fast as the wind,
Children eating soup and potatoes,
Children cooking sausages on a fire,
Rockets explode in the air,
On a frosty freezing dark night,
It's an exciting night but,
Keep your animals safe in a warm house.

Oliver Wilkins (7)
Ashcombe Primary School, Weston-super-Mare

ANIMAL MOVEMENT

Kittens stalk
Puppies walk
Mice creep
Monkeys peep
Horses clop
Bunnies drop
Birds fly
Butterflies die
Ducks float
Fish don't
Snakes slide
Monkeys hide
Swans kiss
People fish
Lions stalk
But
I walk!

Yasmin La Touche (9)
Ashcombe Primary School, Weston-super-Mare

RAINBOW

The showers of rain and the sparkling sun,
Twinkle as the colours go by,
Violet and indigo shine,
People can see the beautiful colours,
Like red and orange,
Where does the rainbow go?
It fades away,
People wish that the rainbow would stay.

Portia Coburn (7)
Ashcombe Primary School, Weston-super-Mare

BONFIRE NIGHT

Rockets are twisting and turning
Bangers are banging
Sausages are sizzling
Sparklers are sparkling
Catherine wheels are spinning
Potatoes are cooking
The bonfire was amazing.

Ryan Tomkins (7)
Ashcombe Primary School, Weston-super-Mare

RAINBOWS

R ain sprinkles, sun shining
A rainbow appears
I t is really nice to see
N o one can stop it from moving
B ig bridge across the sky
O ver the hills
W ill it fade away?

Joshua Farrow (8)
Ashcombe Primary School, Weston-super-Mare

WINTER COMES

Winter comes with rain pattering.
Winter comes with snowflakes glistening.
Winter comes with trees swaying.
Winter comes with little red robins.
Winter comes with me opening presents.
Winter comes with Santa laughing.
Winter ends with the sun coming up.

Chloe Davies (8)
Ashcombe Primary School, Weston-super-Mare

JUMP OR JIGGLE

Lions walk
Pumas stalk

Cheetahs hurry
Lynx scurry

Humpback whales jump
Caterpillars hump

Bees sting
Blue whales sing

Seagulls glide
But I slide down slides.

Evie Redford (8)
Ashcombe Primary School, Weston-super-Mare

CATS

My cat:
Stalks menacingly
Pads softly
Sleeps dreamily
Runs poshly
Yawns slowly
Eats crazily
Growls angrily
Climbs carefully
Purrs quietly
Stretches lazily
Moves creepily
That's my cat!

Lucy Keedwell (8)
Ashcombe Primary School, Weston-super-Mare

WINTER COMES

Winter comes
    with snow falling
Winter comes
    With rain pattering
Winter comes
    With Santa flying
Winter comes
    With rainbows appearing
Winter comes
    With trees waving
Winter comes
    With snowflakes gliding
Winter ends
    When spring comes.

Thomas Sage (9)
Ashcombe Primary School, Weston-super-Mare

CATS

The baby kitten leaps actively.
The ginger cat hunts quietly.
The black cat climbs steadily.
The stripy cat sways gently.
The fat cat eats happily.
The thin cat jumps joyfully.
The mother cat shows off proudly.
The father cat creeps secretly.
The old cat dozes restfully.
The young cat scampers happily,
But I love my cat best.

Tamsin Macbeath (8)
Ashcombe Primary School, Weston-super-Mare

AUTUMN

A ll the leaves are falling gently off the trees
U nder the ground the squirrels hibernate carefully
T iptoe down the streets they go, hunting for some nuts
U ntidy leaves being kicked around on the ground
M e and my friends playing in the leaves
N ow is the time to hide and sleep.

Micah-Josie Denmead (8)
Ashcombe Primary School, Weston-super-Mare

AUTUMN

A utumn leaves are gently falling
U ntidy squirrels throw nuts at you
T rees are swaying in the breeze
U ncolourful leaves fall from the trees
M aple leaves don't taste like syrup
N uts are falling and now I have to go.

Mollie Neal (9)
Ashcombe Primary School, Weston-super-Mare

AUTUMN

A t the park the children play happily.
U p in the trees suddenly conkers fall.
T rees with brown crispy leaves swaying.
U p in the sky the sun shines brightly.
M y friends and me spot squirrels hiding.
N ow it's time to go home.

Laura Escott (8)
Ashcombe Primary School, Weston-super-Mare

Winter Comes

Winter comes
    With lightning flashing
Winter comes
    With snow falling
Winter comes
    With thunder roaring
Winter comes
    With rain pouring
Winter comes
    With puddles splashing
Winter comes
    With people sneezing
Winter comes
    With Santa flying
Winter comes
    With wind blowing
Winter comes
    With children freezing
Winter ends
    With snowdrops growing.

Becky Light (9)
Ashcombe Primary School, Weston-super-Mare

Autumn

A squirrel is scampering across the path
U mbrellas are needed in the autumn
T rees are swaying and leaves are falling
U p on the hill it's very cold now
M y conkers are smashing to bits
N ow autumn's nearly over, winter is on its way.

Emily Tyrrell (9)
Ashcombe Primary School, Weston-super-Mare

WINTER COMES

Winter comes
With wind howling
Winter comes
With leaves falling
Winter comes
With Santa coming
Winter comes
With sky darkening
Winter comes
With heaters warming
Winter comes
With children playing
Winter ends
With warmer days.

Oliver Loud (8)
Ashcombe Primary School, Weston-super-Mare

CATS

My cat:
Climbs carefully
Jumps softly
Runs slowly
Twitches silently
Prowls loudly
Twirls madly
Sleeps happily
Stretches lazily
Purrs slowly
Shows poshly
Pads slyly
That's my cat!

Sarah Knott (8)
Ashcombe Primary School, Weston-super-Mare

EVENING

Evening comes
    with fires flickering.

Evening comes
    with dark clouds gathering.

Evening comes
    with parents chattering boringly.

Evening comes
    with tea cooking steamily.

Evening comes
    with the moon rising slowly.

Evening comes
    with birds singing sweetly.

Evening comes
    with children playing playfully.

Evening comes
    with dads sunbathing sleepily.

Evening comes
    with nurses nursing carefully.

Evening comes
    with animals sleeping.

Evening comes.

Kelsie-Rose Edwards (8)
Ashcombe Primary School, Weston-super-Mare

EVENING

Evening comes
With TVs glowing brightly

Evening comes
With children stamping noisily

Evening comes
With children fighting thunderously

Evening comes
With people exercising stiffly

Evening comes
With crackling fires burning

Evening comes
With people eating peacefully

Evening comes
With the sun setting calmly

Evening comes
With curtains closing swiftly

Evening comes
With people snoring deafeningly

Evening comes
With people reading enjoyably

Evening comes.

Emily Sims (9)
Ashcombe Primary School, Weston-super-Mare

MY CAT

Purrs softly
Leaps energetically
Hunts menacingly
Plays childishly
Pounces swiftly
Spies suspiciously
Sleeps peacefully
Hides secretly
Walks proudly
Yawns sleepily
Prowls silently
That's my cat.

Philip Howe (8)
Ashcombe Primary School, Weston-super-Mare

CATS

My cat:
Purrs loudly
Sleeps quietly
Runs madly
Pads softly
Pounces wildly
Sleeps lazily
Arches proudly
Walks stupidly
Climbs menacingly
Runs energetically
That's my cat!

Elliott Green (8)
Ashcombe Primary School, Weston-super-Mare

WINTER

Winter comes with children snowboarding safely
Winter comes with snowflakes falling gently
Winter comes with ice melting slowly
Winter comes with wind whistling softly
Winter comes with wolves howling loudly
Winter comes with dinner boiling tastily
Winter comes with children playing happily
Winter comes with people skating rapidly
Winter comes.

Charley Hearne (8)
Ashcombe Primary School, Weston-super-Mare

THE STAR

The star that shines so brightly
up high.
The star that lights up
the sky.
The star you'll find that's
always there.
The star that makes you stop
and stare.
This star creates the
heavens above.
This star creates the
soaring dove.

Lauren Brimble (9)
Freshford VC Primary School, Bath

Socks

Socks are loners,
loners are they.
In the washing
machine they stay.
All sad and lonely,
small, dark and gloomy,
in the washing machine all day.

Lauren Hockenhull (9)
Freshford VC Primary School, Bath

The Magic Box
(Based on 'Magic Box' by Kit Wright)

I'll put in the box . . .
Some nice pictures.
I'll put in the box . . .
A gold flower.
I'll put in the box . . .
A red and black ladybird.
I'll put in the box . . .
A purple drink with silver.

Milly Palastre (7)
Freshford VC Primary School, Bath

Monty

He's as black as night,
He's as fat as an elephant,
He's as silly as a monkey
And excitable as a chimpanzee,

He's as dribbly as a newborn baby,
He's as sloppy as mud
And as cute as a kitten.
That's my dog, Monty.

Lily Moffatt (9)
Freshford VC Primary School, Bath

STORM CAT
(Inspired by 'The Mousehole Cat' by Antonia Barber and Nicola Bayley)

The sea is like a storm cat
With claws as sharp as knives
The sea is like a storm cat
The cat with nine lives.

Its whiskers are like twisted twine
Its eyes glow like fire
And when it swims across the sea
It leaves a foamy white line.

It will pounce on fishing boats
As if they were mice
It hides from sun and desert
As if it were made of ice.

At night the village fishermen go out
To find the fish they need.
They hope the catch will be a good one
The family to feed.

And when the cat is purring
The boats are gently rocking;
When not, the harbour holds them safe
And keeps the cat well blocked.

Rossana Padget (9)
Freshford VC Primary School, Bath

THE VEGETARIAN TIGER

A tiger went into
a café
to order a strawberry
frappe.
The waiter's knees
began
to
shake.
The tiger said,
'Good Lord man
you look like a blabbering fake!'
'So you'll be wanting steak then?'
stuttered the small man.
The tiger said,
'No way man! I would never touch ham!
I want a fabulous and delightful
broccoli pie please.'
The waiter looked at him and said a quick
goodbye . . .!

Emily Tucker (9)
Freshford VC Primary School, Bath

MY FOAL

She runs through the fields
Like thunder
She jumps like a mountain goat
Her tail swishes when I lead her
Along the road.

Alice Horler (9)
Freshford VC Primary School, Bath

AROUND THE WORLD

A - Afghanistan being angry.
B - Belgium being bored.
C - Cyprus called Chris.
D - Denmark doing dancing.
E - Egypt with no electricity.
F - France flying.
G - Greece who was greasy.
H - Hungary being hungry.
I - Iceland with imperial mints.
J - Jamaica with a king called Jake.
K - Kafistan who hit with a kane.
L - Lapland who likes lollies.
M - Mexico makes a mate.
N - North Pole who was totally naughty.
O - Ocean who supported Owen.
P - Pakistan who sizzled in a pan.
Q - Queensland who moved quick.
R - Rome driving along rough roads.
S - Siberia smashing at SATs.
T - Thailand who was thin.
U - United States who was ugly.
V - Vietnam who liked Venice.
W - Wales who was walking.
XYZ to finish the world trip!

Christopher Jones (8) & Michael Deane (7)
Kewstoke Primary School, Weston-super-Mare

AWFUL AVOCADO

A was an awful avocado
B bashed it
C cut it
D dropped it
E electrocuted it
F fried it
G grazed it
H hid it
I inspected it
J jumped on it
K kicked it
L licked it
M mixed it
N nipped it
O opened it
P pinched it
Q quarrelled with it
R ripped it
S squeezed it
T tore it
U used it
V vomited over it
W wet it
X X-rayed it
Y yelled at it
Z zipped it up
And that was the end of the awful avocado!

Sophie Jones & Emily Davies (10)
Kewstoke Primary School, Weston-super-Mare

BEST FRIENDS

A is for Alexandra an artist like me.
B is for Betty as clever as can be.
C is for Charley a clever clogs.
D is for Dave who dotes on dogs.
E is for Emily who has a listening ear.
F is for Frankie who has no fear.
G is for Georgie who is really great.
H is for Harry who everyone hates.
I is for Izzy who is always ill.
J is for Juliet, friends with Jill.
K is for Katie who likes to kick a ball.
L is for Lucy who likes to lick a lolly.
M is for Mick and N for Nick.
O is for Ollie and P for Polly.
Q is for Queen a lovely doll.
R is for Rachel eating a roll.
S is for Sophie good at sums.
T is for Tom who loves his tum.
U, V and W, X, Y and Z,
All of my other friends
Are tucked up in bed.

Jennifer Tate & Kayleigh Harris (8)
Kewstoke Primary School, Weston-super-Mare

I'm Going Out

'I'm just going out for a moment.'
'Why?'
'To get bread and jam.'
'Why?'
'Because I'm hungry.'
'Why?'
'Because I haven't eaten all day.'
'Why?'
'Because you haven't given me a minute's peace.'
'Why?'
'Why, why, why, can't you say anything else?'
'What?'

Thomas Heeney (7)
Kewstoke Primary School, Weston-super-Mare

Kat Kenning

Mouse hunter
Bird bringer

Dog hater
Silent waiter

Fast runner
Giant leaper

Stroke lover
Noisy purrer

Warm finder
Lazy sleeper.

Paige Copsey (10) & Rebecca Smart (11)
North Petherton Junior School, Bridgwater

KENNING

Book writer,
Phoney famous,
Pixie lover,
Excuse maker,
Rock smasher,
Mind taker,
Magical me!

Answer: Gilderoy Lockhart.

Jevon Wheeler (11), Ben Woodrow & James Fox (10)
North Petherton Junior School, Bridgwater

THE TANK

Rolling,
Noisy, the tank
Rolls noisily in the forest
As it prepares for desert war
Boom! Boom!

Lee Llewellyn & Joe Ellis (11)
North Petherton Junior School, Bridgwater

CINQUAIN

Porsches
Rolling fast wheels
Speeding up like a dart
Getting faster by the minute
Brakes on!

Philip Prince, Daniel Pike & Patrick McCarthy (11)
North Petherton Junior School, Bridgwater

HEROES

Flying
Along the sky
Spotting troops on the ground
Its machine guns are firing.
All clear.

Landing
Troops moving out
Taking cover by rocks
Firing . . . firing . . .
Fire!

Their goals
Land by copter
Find the missing hostages
Take out all the enemy troops
Simple.

Cave found
Enemy troops
SAS shoot them all
Allied hostages in the cave
Help them.

Armoured
Car arriving
The war is not over
Going to a safe location
Rescued.

Robert Sturgeon (10)
North Petherton Junior School, Bridgwater

GUESS WHO?

Champion-leaper
Food-seeker
Claw-scratcher
Sun-sleeper
Mouse-hunter
Lap-curler
Fluffy-stroker
Bin-trasher.

(A - A cat)

Kathleen Bullock (10) & Hayley Duddridge (11)
North Petherton Junior School, Bridgwater

A CAT

Mouse catcher
Sly snatcher

Silent walker
Sly stalker

Whisker wearer
Fine sharer

High leaper
Dozy sleeper.

Laura Flaherty (11)
North Petherton Junior School, Bridgwater

Pylons

The big grey metal man,
prisoners striding across the land.
Sounds like eggs being fried,
fizzing and fuzzing.
Standing straight like soldiers in uniform
high towards the clouds they stand.
They hold their chains with their powerful arms.
Don't touch their hands, they're fully charged!

Jacob Gamble (9)
Norton Fitzwarren CE VC Community School, Taunton

Maize Giants

Maize giants stand in rows
like armies preparing for battle.
The jungle-like maize swirling in the wind
when big coal trains go jetting by
with the rush of the wind against it.

Ben Jewell (10)
Norton Fitzwarren CE VC Community School, Taunton

Whispering Ghosts

Smooth whispering white ghosts
Snapping green maize
Long and strong grey bones
Hearts lift upon the sky
Thinking someone's died.

Jessie Smith (10)
Norton Fitzwarren CE VC Community School, Taunton

BROKEN SILENCE

Soldiers standing under light breeze.
A big metal giant standing tall
Under the grey autumn day.
Dark shoots stabbing out of the ground,
A never-ending jungle ahead.
Dancing corn in the field
A tipsy silent stream
A grey, never-ending, boring day.
High clouds rise as time ticks by,
A skeleton standing tall with pride
A train shoots past like an arrow.
A waving swaying driver
Tears through the silence of the day.

Lee Phillips (10)
Norton Fitzwarren CE VC Community School, Taunton

BY THE RIVERSIDE

Ripples rip the dingy river,
Silent as the drowning leaves
That slowly swirl like a sinking boat
Swirling as the wind goes round
Rushing down the winding river
As I see the leaves go down
Swaying trees over the river
Trying to float as they sink.
If you listen you will hear
The trains roaring like a tiger
Zooming like a red arrow
Disturbing the peace as it goes by.

Olivia Baggley (10)
Norton Fitzwarren CE VC Community School, Taunton

THE OCEAN OF TREES

A scary crispy whisper swims
In the slapping, flapping sea of maize,
Its waving, nodding tipsy tops
Are swaying like the ocean waves.
Its corn cob hiding like fat brown snakes,
The bubbling dark river floating down.
Its tangled alley of trees and weeds
Branches paddling in the murky water.

Ryan Hallett (9)
Norton Fitzwarren CE VC Community School, Taunton

SEASONS

Autumn days maize forest
Skeletal horizon whispering ghosts.
Maize stands tall, like soldiers strong
Metal man marching. Grey
Winter's cold whispering days.

Josh Williams (9)
Norton Fitzwarren CE VC Community School, Taunton

THE FOREST

Maize as tall as a human
on a grey autumn day.
It looks like a nodding forest,
leaves like strips of bright green paper.
They sound like whispering ghosts
wavy, bendy, dancing forest.

Josh Summers (9)
Norton Fitzwarren CE VC Community School, Taunton

AN AUTUMN DAY

The powerful river sneaks through the land
like a lion stalking his prey.
A crystal waterfall, slapping and churning
the smooth glowing surface.
As the sunlight shines, the river sparkles
and the waterfall glitters and gleams.
Slowly the water slips away
into the autumn trees.

Grass swayed by a gentle breeze
and farmers' fields ploughed.
Crispy brown leaves ready to fall
and a tired green landscape.
Gangs of nettles ready to sting
and a drift of camomile flowers.
Little flies jiggle in the air
like tiny puppets dancing.

Leanne Robertson (10)
Norton Fitzwarren CE VC Community School, Taunton

AUTUMN DAYS

The sad grey days of autumn have begun,
nothing growing now in these dismal fields.
Electric lines fizzing in the breeze,
rivers ripple beneath the gloomy trees,
gushing water thundering down the weir,
gangs of nettles attacking passers-by.
Metal monsters standing tall and strong,
wild ragwort growing on the mud ramps,
lumpy, milk chocolate-coloured earth.

Christopher Manuel (11)
Norton Fitzwarren CE VC Community School, Taunton

THE WALK

The glum ploughed earth, like powdered chocolate,
Its golden crop now long-forgotten,
Camomile flower as white as snow.
A bumpy log that leads to a field
Where the eely river thunders down its falls,
Bubbling to the surface from the greasy ground,
To creep away through the overgrowth,
Its ripples giggling across its skin.

Jordan Hawkins (10)
Norton Fitzwarren CE VC Community School, Taunton

THE STREAM

The slow stream sneaks across the farmer's fields,
The wild waterfall whizzes in the pale pool,
The lazy leaf falls quietly into the pale pool,
A dopey dog barks badly at the slippery stick,
The wet wellies splash and smash the slow stream,
The slow stream slowly drifts away.

Terri Joyner (10)
Norton Fitzwarren CE VC Community School, Taunton

CHAMPAGNE BUBBLE BATH

A champagne bubble bath fizzes beneath the weir,
brandy dark its dismal pool,
sunlight glimmers over secretive waters,
glittery ripples slowly drifting.

Feathery leaves rustling on the bank,
a drift of freshness in the air,
the fall as cold and white as icicles.
A hint of winter is on its way.

Jessica Sillett (11)
Norton Fitzwarren CE VC Community School, Taunton

THE PYLONS

Tall metal Martians
like an army of soldiers,
fuzzing and buzzing
they carry electric power,
enormous statues joined by
handcuffs as they stomp,
massive aliens invading the Earth
as patient slaves to us.

Kristopher Speechly (9)
Norton Fitzwarren CE VC Community School, Taunton

THE RIVER

In the sneaky shy river
Twitchy ripples twirl
And bumbling jumbling water swirls.
Weeping willow hangs.
Fish sleep in their gritty beds.
On beyond the river a clumsy waterfall.
Where vines of water dangles.

Olivia Pring (9)
Norton Fitzwarren CE VC Community School, Taunton

PYLONS

The sound is like brothers in arms
Buzzing furiously in the rain.
Keeps lights shining in our homes,
Wire wrapped up like a cone.

Buzz, buzz, buzz like a swarm of bees
Breathing air from the wind.
Always getting ready to battle
Like a big swarm of cattle.

Silver metal, thin and hard,
Skinny arms that stretch out straight.
Clutching veins that buzz with power,
Moving round them hour by hour.

Jessica Cornish (10)
Norton Fitzwarren CE VC Community School, Taunton

PYLONS

On a dim, dark, grey, gloomy day
The massive, mighty, metal, monstrous men
They make a loud fizzing noise
They are towering up and away
They're linked together with just a piece of wire
Massive soldiers bring power to our houses
Falling down because of the wild wind
Crushing people to death when they stumble down
Go too close to them and you will get shocked.
Pylons - *massive, mighty, metal, monstrous men.*

Daniel Cooke (10)
Norton Fitzwarren CE VC Community School, Taunton

9TH OCTOBER

Autumn's dim and chilly weather.
Gloomy clouds cover the sun.
Jiggling flies around your head.
Puppets on invisible strings!

Skinny pylons seem to stride
Across the milky chocolate earth.
As shadowy river flexes its muscles,
As strong currents rise, boil.
The river's as slippery as an eel.

Ripples like a turtle shell.
The weir is filled with bubbling noise.
Trees talking over the rocks.

Kirsty Mabley (10)
Norton Fitzwarren CE VC Community School, Taunton

THE RIVER

In behind the hidden den
Crashing down the waterfall
Drifting across the fresh stream
Highlighting vines of water
Where the weeping willow hangs
Champagne froth scatters elsewhere
Crazy, clumsy waterfall
Flimsy leaves flow gently
Loud thundering, bumbling
Plunging into deep depths.

Charlotte Callun (9)
Norton Fitzwarren CE VC Community School, Taunton

AN OLD CREEPY MAZE

An old spooky maze with old metal men
Birds pecking sweetcorn in the creepy maze
Crispy leaves flapping above me up high
Like a wishing star coming down towards my side
Like a robin swooping.

Tiffany Rustage (8)
Norton Fitzwarren CE VC Community School, Taunton

RIVER

An autumn day at the silver river,
Flowing gently around the dull stony island.
Milk melted chocolate and bubbles.

Green fields with dancing flies.
Leafy rocks with damp banks.
Dogs barking in the river.

Amy Bond (9)
Norton Fitzwarren CE VC Community School, Taunton

THE DREAMY STREAM

The dreamy stream comes drifting down
over the twinkling chilly waters,
above their steep and stony depths
reflected sun makes faces shine,
highlights skin and hair with gold.

The glassy waterfall flickers its power,
as bubbly bobbles rise from beneath
floating leaves fall from the tops
softly dimpling the river skin.

Jade Groody (10)
Norton Fitzwarren CE VC Community School, Taunton

FIELD OF SOLDIERS

A maize as tall as soldiers
On a grey autumn days.
Baby plants shooting from the ground
The wind as loud as ghosts.
The trees swaying like a drunken sailor.

Rhys Sykes (9)
Norton Fitzwarren CE VC Community School, Taunton

AUTUMN DAYS

A sad grey autumn day,
The river spinning slowly down,
Long and lush leaves floating by,
The river twisting peacefully,
The maize dancing beautifully,
A light whisper comes from the maize.

Naomi Williams (11)
Norton Fitzwarren CE VC Community School, Taunton

BATTLEFIELD OF SOLDIERS

A fish is hiding in the reflections
In the direction of the sea
Maize stands like soldiers, waiting
On a desert battlefield.
Maizes shivering in the darkness
Of the dark, black, scary sky.
Rabbits hopping in the sun, like children
Excited on Christmas Eve.
Birds singing in the trees, like a big
Brass band of men. I hear a train like
A thunderstorm, dashing like an atomic bomb.

Josh Mattravers (9)
Norton Fitzwarren CE VC Community School, Taunton

RIVER

A dull grey ceiling of dusky sky
down by the river with its powerful current.
Feathery trees hanging over the sunlit water.

Slippery rocks as slippy as can be.
Champagne bubbles dotted around,
Looks hot but is very cold!

Beware you never know what's
Lurking at the bottom!

Slithering eels and slippery fish!

Gemma Dalton (11)
Norton Fitzwarren CE VC Community School, Taunton

WHAT IS RED!

What is red? Blood is red
Bleeding in my bed.

What is blue? Water is blue
With fish swimming through.

What is green? My book is,
Like leaves are green.

What is white? The paper's white
When we may write.

What is brown? A tree trunk is brown,
When the king gets his crown.

Ross Ashman (9)
Oldfield Park Junior School, Bath

THE DOG

He is as tall as a three-year-old,
As brave as a lion,
As gentle as a lamb
And is fast like a cheetah.

He's always there when I'm sad,
He is never ever bad,
His fur is black like shoe polish
And his fur is like a cushion
And his name is Duke.

Rebecca Wall (8)
Oldfield Park Junior School, Bath

WRITING A POEM

'Right then everyone you have 30 minutes to write a poem,
About anything you like!'
30 minutes to write a poem!
On your bloomin' bike!
I'm just going to sit here and let time pass,
Just like the rest of the class!
But the teacher's coming over
To look at what I've done!
I quickly scribble down something for fun!
'Well done Billy,' Mrs Jones said.
'But next time don't write in red!'
Well that's my poem finished now,
It's nearly half-past three.
So I'll leave it in this book
For you all to see!

James Butt (10)
Oldfield Park Junior School, Bath

MOTOR CROSS

M otorbikes revving, ready to go,
O ff they go! Around the corners and up the jumps
T rying to stay on the bike,
O ver the jump they fly,
R ound the corner one falls off.

C up is waiting for the winner,
R evving the bike they're near the end,
O il's burning really fast,
S taying on the bike a man overtakes,
S trike! Number 4 has won.

Andrew Bean (10)
Oldfield Park Junior School, Bath

MY BROTHER

My brother is annoying,
He really is a pain,
He always torments me,
He messes with my brain.
He comes in my room and takes my stuff,
I said, 'Give it back.'
He said, 'Tough.'
He embarrasses me when he is rude
And when he drinks and eats his food.
I try to avoid him but he gets in my way,
My brother is always there, I put up with him all day,
It's worse when there is double, when he has a guest,
But my brother is my brother, he truly is the best!

Holly Lakeman (10)
Oldfield Park Junior School, Bath

HURRICANE

Hurricane! Hurricane!
It's on the mountain,
I know it's there,
It's so strong, rubbish is already flying in the air,
Coming closer every second,
I can see it, I'm watching it through the attic window,
It's on the hills,
I can hear it,
It's right by us on the ground,
We're going to get hit,
Oh no!
It's got us.

Oliver Ashley-Owen (9)
Oldfield Park Junior School, Bath

COLOURS

Lions are as yellow as a pot of paint.
Bears are as brown as people's eyes.
Grasshoppers bounce like a kangaroo.
Snakes are as green as grass
And a fish is as orange as an orange.

Scott Jardine (9)
Oldfield Park Junior School, Bath

THE BATTERING RAM

Fluffy like a cloud,
Head like a rock,
Horns like a helter-skelter,
This creature likes to ram things.
I wouldn't like to be with it,
When it gets mad it's as fast a stampeding buffalo.

Laurence Kemp (8)
Oldfield Park Junior School, Bath

MY TARANTULA POEM

My tarantula bites,
It'll chew you,
It's black,
It's got a black cage,
I'll give it a bath,
My tarantula.

Damien Evered (9)
Oldfield Park Junior School, Bath

THE DRAGON

Eyes as red and orange as fire,
Claws as long as (twice) the size of cats.
Teeth as sharp as a butcher's knife,
Breath as hot as the scorching desert.
Body as round as a hot air balloon,
Fierce as a shark.
Green as dark green grass,
Long scales as sharp as needles and pins.

Chevenell McRae (9)
Oldfield Park Junior School, Bath

MY FUNNY CAT

My cat's eyes are like small balls.
His fur is as soft as the clouds.
Little paws as small as mice.
His fur is brown and orange.
As fat as a pig.
He likes to hide in our rooms
And he headbutts you if you put your head near him.

Jessica Asquith-Dagger (9)
Oldfield Park Junior School, Bath

THE CAT

Fur like silk,
But he's rough and tough.
Paws like ice cubes,
Teeth like steel,
He even likes a good old meal.

Sam Light (9)
Oldfield Park Junior School, Bath

FLOWERS

Red is the colour of a rose
Striking a beautiful pose.

Blue is the colour of a bluebell
With a lovely scented smell.

White is the colour of a snowdrop,
Their heads all dangle and flop.

Yellow is the colour of a sunflower,
Tall and slim like the Eiffel Tower.

Orange is the colour of a marigold
With its head so bright and bold.

Purple is the colour of lavender,
My favourite colour.

Natasha Harris (9)
Oldfield Park Junior School, Bath

MY MONSTER

My monster is very smelly,
As smelly as a tramp.
My monster is very big,
As big as a giant.
I don't like it, it's really too big.
It lived in the cupboard
Until it was too big.
It ate all the food.
My monster is fat,
As big as the world.
My monster smashed the house . . .

Josh Southard Williams (9)
Oldfield Park Junior School, Bath

WHERE ARE YOU SLEEPING NOW?

Where are you sleeping now?

Are you sleeping somewhere hot?
    You always liked the warmest spot!
Are you sleeping somewhere cold?
    You never liked the winter snow!
Are you sleeping in a plant pot?
    You always slept curled up in a ball!
Are you sleeping on a path?
    You quite often sat in the bath!
Are you on a beanbag?
    You always liked a comfy spot!
Are you under a bush?
    Your favourite spot was the rhubarb bush!
That's how you got your name
    My very special ginger friend!
        My cat Rhubarb!

Hannah Woodland (10)
Oldfield Park Junior School, Bath

THE GOBBLER

He's got eyes as big as saucers,
A nose as red as a rose,
As naughty as my brother,
Fierce like a shark,
As scary as a spider,
(It even drinks cider),
As fat as a well-fed hippo,
As tall as the tallest giant
And look out, here he comes, aarrgghh!

Olivia Dellow (8)
Oldfield Park Junior School, Bath

BUSTER!

Eyes as big as a hippo,
Nose as small as a button on a shirt.
Teeth as sharp as a needle,
Fur as fluffy as a teddy bear.
His bark is like a mouse's squeak,
Stares like nobody wants him.
His ears are droopy as if they're falling off.

Oh Buster!

Gemma Eades (8)
Oldfield Park Junior School, Bath

BUSTER!

Eyes as blue as the sea,
Nose like a little black button.
Mouth as sad as a little girl's cry,
Staring 'cause nobody wants me.
Fur as brown as chocolate,
Teeth as sharp as a pin.
His bark like a mouse's squeak,
His ears as pink as a mouse's ears.

Oh Buster!

Adele Wallis-Poulton (8)
Oldfield Park Junior School, Bath

MY CAT GARFIELD

Garfield is as nice as the sun,
He's like a gentle cloud
Who wouldn't hurt a fly,
He always likes to lay on my lap asleep.

Garfield, he always miaows as soft as me,
He would always like me to feed him
Because he likes me so much,
That's my cat Garfield.

Holly Aldous (9)
Oldfield Park Junior School, Bath

MONSTER POEM

As fat as an elephant,
As sporty as Beckham,
As cold as ice,
As white as snow,
As big as a giant,
As funny as a comedian,
As active as a runner,
Now as still as a rock,
Bye monster!

Nathan Gormley (9)
Oldfield Park Junior School, Bath

THE CROCODILE

Green like grass,
Teeth like swords,
Eyes as dark as the night,
As long as a train
Or an aeroplane,
Mouth as big as a bird,
Eats like a hippo.

Daniel Ashworth (8)
Oldfield Park Junior School, Bath

IF
(Based on 'If' by Rudyard Kipling)

If you can do all the maths right
    And your teacher is proud of you.
If you can have a great time at school
    And forget about the fun at home.
If you can make the time go quickly
    With a lot of excitement from play.
If you can get all your work done in time
    And do the finisher's fun work.
If you pay attention to the teachers in class
    Or in the assembly too.

If you can learn something new every day
    Or learn a bit more of the subject you've done this week.
If you can do what the golden rules say
    Without breaking any at all.
If you can face the big bullies
    And not torment them back.
If you like school that much
    And do everything on this list,

You will definitely succeed!

Gemma Broad (10)
Oldfield Park Junior School, Bath

HOLLY

Hair like sand, as long as an elephant's trunk,
Eyes the colour of a light sea,
As fast as a great white shark after its prey,
As pretty as a coloured butterfly,
Bright and happy like the sun,
That's my friend Holly.

Florence Hinton-Collyer (8)
Oldfield Park Junior School, Bath

WHERE ARE YOU NOW?

Are you walking somewhere hot?
Are you jogging on the spot?
Are you walking in the town?
Are you falling down?
Are you in an aeroplane?
Are you eating on the train?
Are you sleeping somewhere cold?
Are you treading in some mould?
Are you doing work at school?
Are you splashing in a pool?
Are you reading a book?
Are you on the look?
Are you eating yummy food?
Are you in a happy mood?
Are you in a field?
Are you dressing up with a shield,
Or are just at home sleeping all alone?

Catherine Bradbeer (10)
Oldfield Park Junior School, Bath

THE BULLY

Fists like clay,
Voice like thunder,
Temper like a lion's,
Tall as a giraffe,
Big as a whale,
But deep down inside
I know he's just a coward.

Josh Catchpool (9)
Oldfield Park Junior School, Bath

WHAT IS RED?

What is red? A rose is red
In his little bed.
What is blue? The sea is blue
Where fish swim through.
What is white? The cloud is white
Sailing through the light.
What is yellow? A buttercup is yellow,
What a jolly fellow.
What is green? The grass is green
With buttercups between.
What is brown? A bench is brown
In the town.

Callum Ball (9)
Oldfield Park Junior School, Bath

THE LIVERPOOL POEM

Santa left me many gifts,
Far too many for me to list
But what did I like best of all?
I put it on to play football.
The shorts are blue,
The socks are green,
The shirt's the best I've ever seen.
The kit of, course, is for Liverpool,
My favourite football team.
I'd like to go and see them play
But that's a present for my birthday!

Kyle Norris (10)
Oldfield Park Junior School, Bath

MY HOLIDAY

I'm always excited about my holiday,
We leave to go on a Saturday.
We go for a week,
But it's usually very bleak.
The journey is very long
And on the way we sing a song.
We have a competition on who can see the sea,
Will it be him or will it be me?
We finally arrive,
It's been a long drive.
Hooray the sun is shining in the sky,
The tide is in,
So we go for a swim.

David Locke (10)
Oldfield Park Junior School, Bath

WHO AM I?

I have a wife and one daughter,
I am a rapper,
I have several different albums,
I have a partner called Dr Dre,
I have held loads of concerts,
I've just starred in a new film,
I sometimes team up with D12,
I've just released a new song,
I've got some collectable dolls of me . . .
I am Eminem.

Craig Wall (10)
Oldfield Park Junior School, Bath

ABOUT ME

Lauren Blackmore is my name,
I'm not very good at writing,
I like getting stuck in a book
And reading about people fighting.

I hang around with Becky,
She is really, really kind,
She said she wears braces
And wishes they were mine.

I have a brother called Sam
And sometimes he can be a pain,
But wherever he goes he is always the same.

I like singing songs
And talking about things,
But when I'm really busy
I hear the phone ring.

When I'm in the playground
I hear the school bell,
I rush into the classroom
Hoping they won't tell.

When I get home from school
I listen to my music,
Singing to the songs even if I hate it.

When we go out shopping
I go a bit over the top,
I buy all these things
And stuff I should have not.

I'm not your normal average girl,
I'm not into ponies or a hairdo,
But somehow I always end up in a shop
Buying trousers and a top too.

Lauren Blackmore (11)
Oldfield Park Junior School, Bath

THE LOST PUPPY

Walking along the street,
A lost puppy got to its feet.
With my hand I stroked,
To my amazement my love I proved.

His fur was dirty and matted,
It was as though it had been plaited.
His body was ever so thin,
To go without food was a sin.

I took him under my wing
And taught him how to sing.
At home I gave him a bath,
Together we had a good laugh.

He ate me out of my home,
No matted fur, I brushed him with a comb.
He was, after time, very healthy,
Although I was not very wealthy.

We sleep together in my bed,
My hand rested upon his head.
When he wakes up from his sleep,
He's mine now, mine to keep.

Amy North (10)
Oldfield Park Junior School, Bath

WHILE WALKING

While walking through the centre of town who was I to see?
Many familiar faces all staring at me.
I wondered if I had seen them before walking in a three,
But then I remembered names: Sam, Ben and Lee.
Sam was a good friend and had the fastest legs ever,
He claimed that all his speed came from his lucky feather.
Ben was a bit older and a bit wiser too,
He would think before acting and be faithful and true.
While Lee was very tall and was a very good friend
And if you didn't have it he would happily lend.
While walking through town this is whom I saw,
Sam, Ben and Lee on a guided tour.

Laurence Murray (11)
Oldfield Park Junior School, Bath

PEOPLE IN THE PARK

People are in the park playing all day,
Getting in the way,
Taken with your brother
And all your family like your mother.
Your dad takes you on the swing,
It's like flying with wings.
As I whizz down the slide,
Through the bushes my brother hides.
Climbing up the climbing frame,
'Hip hip hooray,' I say.
The gate has closed, home is away,
I'll be back another day.

William Robinson (10)
Oldfield Park Junior School, Bath

THE BULLY

I sit in the corner of the playground,
Really scared, waiting for the bully to come round.
I hear heavy footsteps coming closer and closer to me.
I close my eyes tightly, thinking that it's him but it's not,
It's my dad coming to collect me.
I breathe a huge sigh of relief, I'm okay until tomorrow.

Jessica Archer (10)
Oldfield Park Junior School, Bath

MY CAT

As fat as an elephant,
As black as night,
As slow as a slug,
As big as a building,
As greedy as a bug,
It's my cat.

Sam Meopham (8)
Oldfield Park Junior School, Bath

MONSTER POEM

As white as the snow,
Eyes as blue as the sea,
Spotty as a leopard,
Teeth as sharp as a knife,
As swift as a tiger,
The monster!

Benjamin Laslett (8)
Oldfield Park Junior School, Bath

MY HAMSTER

My hamster is as furry as a hare,
He has sharp teeth like a bear.

My hamster is as fast as lightning,
He can get from here to Bristol in a *ping*.

My hamster is as good as gold,
He does what he is told.

My hamster is brown and white,
But my hamster does not bite.

My hamster lives in a cage,
He does a dance on top of the stage.

My hamster is called Fudge.

Emma Walker (9)
Oldfield Park Junior School, Bath

THERE'S SOMETHING IN THE CUPBOARD

There's something in the cupboard,
It's eating all the food,
It's as fat as an elephant,
It's as greedy as a pig.
It jumps at you all the time,
It's as fierce as a shark.
It smells like a dead skunk
And its teeth could get through metal.
Its feet are as big as a house,
Its nose is as big as itself.

Peter Sixsmith (9)
Oldfield Park Junior School, Bath

ROSE

A tiny seed that has been sown
Has been watered and slowly grown.

The roots burst out and burrow underground
Not making a single sound.

The sprout peeps up into the light
And stays there watching overnight.

The stem grows slim, but strong and tall
Supported by the solid wall.

Petals stretch out and show bright red,
Camouflaged against the wall by its flower bed.

People freeze to watch and stare
To see the beauty that lays there.

Morwenna Harrington (10)
Oldfield Park Junior School, Bath

WHAT AM I?

Best flyer,
Food spyer,
Cocoon spinner,
Nectar eater,
Caterpillar changer,
What am I?

Sky glider,
Pollen sucker,
What am I?
A butterfly of course!

Jessica Ball (10)
Oldfield Park Junior School, Bath

THE STAR

The star is bright in the moonlight,
Shining in the darkness like a light.
When night falls a star appears and thousands come,
Big stars glow and small stars shine,
Most stick but some fall.
The burning balls of gas are so far away you cannot see them glow.
Twinkling and shimmering.

Georgia Sheppard (10)
Oldfield Park Junior School, Bath

T-REX

Meat eater,
Clumsy animal,
Hairy beast,
Tailed creature,
Man eater,
Strong teeth,
Large nostrils,
Sharp nails,
Large brain,
Tough legs,
Weak arms,
Strong back,
Amazing eyesight,
Excellent killer,
Brilliant hunter,
Bone crusher,
Powerful kicker.

Aaron Farnham (10)
Oldfield Park Junior School, Bath

SUN

I am very bright,
I make the day very light.

I come up in the morning
While people are still yawning.

While people are still in their beds
Resting their sleepyheads.

I am making the city hot
Just like the cooker with the stew pot.

Sometimes I get really mad
Then I go from good to bad.

Sometimes I like to kill,
But when the snow comes I get a really bad chill.

Serena Wall (9)
Oldfield Park Junior School, Bath

ROBBER

Good runner,
Jewel lover,
Good designer,
Stripy top wearer,
Jail breaker,
Terrible smoker,
Money stealer,
Police hider,
Good sneaker,
Tiptoe creeper.

Kieran Cox (9)
Oldfield Park Junior School, Bath

LAMBORGHINIS

L ong as a Mitsubishi Lancer,
A very big exhaust pipe,
M ph is faster than a Ferrari,
B righter than the sun,
O ut of the city in less than three minutes,
R ound wheels,
G rowls like a lion,
H exagonal headlights,
I mportant to a racing car owner,
N eat leather seats,
I ce-cold air conditioning,
S afe as a bank.

Iqubal Hussain (9)
Oldfield Park Junior School, Bath

TODDLER

Nose picker,
Toy player,
Big crier,
Small stander,
Big whiner,
Puppy dog eyes,
Noise maker,
Toy breaker,
Puddle splasher,
Dummy lover,
Stone thrower.

Seb Burvill (10)
Oldfield Park Junior School, Bath

CATS AND DOGS

I sat and ate my dinner
One very sunny day,
When I heard a rumbling noise
Coming from my way.

I got up and looked about
But saw no silly trouble,
When I thought to sit back down
I realised I had double!

My dog Shelly and my cat
Were rushing down the hall.
Shelly close on Chloe's tail
Swiping with one paw.

Claire Kingwell (10)
Oldfield Park Junior School, Bath

I WON'T GET UP

I know I have to get up,
But I'm superglued to my bed!
If I don't my mum will get a cup
And pour water all over my head.

Now I'm really wet,
Oh no my sister's coming into my room,
She's like a noisy pet.
Now I've met my doom
Maybe I will get up!

Rachel Eades (10)
Oldfield Park Junior School, Bath

THE AFRICAN CUB

He is asleep in the long grass
Licking his paws and dreaming,
Dreaming about catching his prey.
When he wakes up
He sees another cub,
This time it is a girl,
The girl is called Ella.
Ella and the African cub begin to play,
They have to go home,
It is time to return to their mum.

Matthew Arthurs (9)
Oldfield Park Junior School, Bath

MANCHESTER UNITED

Fast runners,
Red wearers,
Quick passers,
Beckham supporters,
Corner takers,
Foul makers,
Good free kickers,
Super savers,
Offside do-ers,
Strong lobbers,
Red Devil players.

Thomas Fry (10)
Oldfield Park Junior School, Bath

LIMERICKS

I was washing my hands in the bathroom
When I spotted my mum had lost the broom.
So I went out in a hurry
Not stopping for a curry
Till I found her sitting in gloom.

I was looking out the window at the moon
When my mum said, 'Go to bed soon.'
I replied I was bored,
So I got out my sword,
Then she suddenly shouted, 'Room!'

Samuel Melbourne (8)
Oldfield Park Junior School, Bath

MY RABBIT

R   abbits are my very favourite animal
A   nd my rabbit is white,
B   ut sometimes he is messy,
B   y the time he is cleaned he is messy again.
I   really like my rabbit, I think he is the best.
T   oday I went to see my rabbit because he isn't in my back garden yet as he lives next door at the moment. We are getting him next week but he is still mine!

Sophie Burman (10)
Oldfield Park Junior School, Bath

WHAT AM I?

I live under the sea,
I cannot fly like a bee,
I am yellow and a nice fellow,
I am not a fish,
I like to snuggle in the sand,
But I do not like coming on land,
When sharks come by
I either hide or cry,
I can't walk,
I can't talk,
I'm quite small
And not very tall,
I like to wriggle,
I like to giggle,
Have you guessed what I am yet?

A starfish!

Jessica Newman (9)
Oldfield Park Junior School, Bath

A RIDDLE - WHAT AM I?

I sparkle in the light,
I am able to fly,
People look up to see me,
I love Christmas time,
I rest on trees,
I hold a stick but not to help me walk,
Magic follows me around.

Who am I?

Emily Whittock (9)
Oldfield Park Junior School, Bath

MY CATS

My cats are called Darley and Pushey.
They eat all day and sleep all day in a cat house.
They always beg for food when there is already some.
Darley is ginger and Pushey is black-grey.
They are both brothers.
They are seven.
They are great.

Sam Hughes (9)
Oldfield Park Junior School, Bath

MY HORSE

My horse is as black as midnight,
She has a long white mane as white as snow.
My horse's eyes are sparkly like diamonds,
She has a long tail as smooth as polar bears' skin.
My horse has lips like mine,
My horse has ears as smooth as a teddy.
She has arms like velvet,
She has eyelashes like brooms.
My horse is *Polo!*

Emma Miller (9)
Oldfield Park Junior School, Bath

HORSE

Horses are fun, they run like the wind,
They are as soft as a teddy,
Their eyes are like sparkling stars,
Their tails are like gold dust,
Their eyelashes are as glittery as silver and gold.

Jessie Banks (8)
Oldfield Park Junior School, Bath

MY CAT

My cat is as good as gold.
My cat's fur is like a sheep's fur
Its tail is as long as a snake.
My cat's ears are pointed like a knife.
My cat is as fast as the speed of light.
She's as small as an ant.
My cat is as white as snow.
She's called Snowy.

Abigail Strange (8)
Oldfield Park Junior School, Bath

DRAGON

D ragon's fire can blow down a castle,
R ed as a flame in your fire
A nd it is enormous and scaly.
G o on and defeat the dragon,
O n the dragon was a crown,
N o one could defeat the dragon.

Jordan Short (10)
Oldfield Park Junior School, Bath

WHAT IS RED?

What is red? Blood is red
Falling out of my head.

What is green? An apple is green,
Green as can be.

What is blue? The sky is blue
Above me and you.

What is white? A swan is white
Sailing on a lake in the sunlight.

Tom Lakeman & Michael Cook (8)
Oldfield Park Junior School, Bath

MONSTER

M ad eater,
O ld monster,
N asty killer,
S nake seeker,
T error to all,
E asy killer,
R ight nasty monster!

Zoë Macey (9)
Oldfield Park Junior School, Bath

WHAT IS GOLD?

What is red? Blood is red
Falling out of your head.
What is blue? The sky is blue
With birds flying through.
What is green? My book is green
And it's very, very clean.
What is gold? Gold is gold,
Gold why just gold.

Daniel Renwick (8)
Oldfield Park Junior School, Bath

WHAT IS WHITE?

What is white? Snow is white,
Made to have a snowball fight.

What is red? My pillow's red
Where I rest my sleepy head.

What is blue? The sky is blue
With aeroplanes flying through.

What is yellow? The sun is yellow
Shining at the world below.

What is green? The grass is green
With little bugs in-between.

What is violet? The classroom is violet
With children being quiet.

What is orange? Why an orange is orange,
Just orange.

Jacob Ives (8)
Oldfield Park Junior School, Bath

WHAT IS WHITE?

What is white? The snow is white when you have a snowball fight.
What is red? A rose is red in its little flower bed.
What is green? Grass is green, to the fields I have been.
What is blue? A shoe is blue when you put it on you.
What is violet? The sky is violet when it twinkles in its twilight.
What is pink? A pen is pink when you colour in so neat.
What is yellow? The sun is yellow, he's a jolly little fellow.

Charleigh Fry (9)
Oldfield Park Junior School, Bath

WHAT IS BLUE?

What is blue? The sea is blue
Waiting for me and you.

What is white? The snow is white
Drifting down for a snowball fight.

What is red? Blood is red
Going through your head.

What is green? The grass is green
With flowers in-between.

What is pink? A rose is pink
Leaning on the sink.

Emily Tolley (9)
Oldfield Park Junior School, Bath

WHAT IS GREEN?

What is green? The grass is green
Like a green bean.

What is yellow? A buttercup is yellow
Like a golden mellow.

What is red? A poppy is red
Like the blood in my head.

What is blue? The sea is blue
With water running through.

Jasmine White (8)
Oldfield Park Junior School, Bath

HANDWRITING

Oh no! It's time for handwriting,
That means it's time to start biting
My pencil on the end.
Now it's time to send
My work to Mrs George.
'Oh no! My handwriting is terrible!
It's the end,' I cried.
'What's the matter?' a kid asked.
'My handwriting!' I replied.
'Good luck,' the kid said.
'I knew I should have stayed in bed,' I sighed.
I'm now finally at Mrs George's office.
She asked, 'What are you doing here? Got into trouble?'
'No, it's my handwriting,' I replied.
'I love it,' she said.
'Huh! My teacher hates it.'
'Oh do it until your teacher likes it.'
Oh no! It's time for handwriting again,
Now I'm back to biting my pencil.

Philip Durham (9)
Oldfield Park Junior School, Bath

A LIMERICK

I was searching in my grandad's storeroom
When a ghost offered me some perfume
So I shouted out, 'Boo!'
What else could I do?
But he couldn't have been real I presume.

Chelsea Buchan (8)
Oldfield Park Junior School, Bath

COLOURS

What is yellow?
The sun is yellow shining in the sky.
What is red?
My curtains are red waiting to be closed.
What is black?
The blackboard is black that Mrs Davis writes on.
What is blue?
The spelling book is blue that we write in.
What is white?
The cloud is white floating through the sky.
What is green?
The grass is green, being cut, smelling sweet.
What is purple?
My plants are purple on the back of leaves.
What is pink?
A pig is pink in its sty.

Verity Bean (9)
Oldfield Park Junior School, Bath

MY CAT

My cat is as good as gold.
Her tail is as long as a snake.

My cat's fur is like a sheep's fur.
She is as white as snow.

My cat's ears are pointed like a knife.
She's as small as an ant.

She's as slow as a tortoise.
She's called Rose.

Charlotte Lakeman (8)
Oldfield Park Junior School, Bath

WHAT AM I?

I am black
And furry.
I love to
Be looked after
And I play
A lot.
When you are
Asleep
I sneak in
And jump on
Your bed and
Fall asleep.
I like lots
Of milk and
I eat a lot.
I am good
At running.
I love to
Pounce on
You.
I purr when
You are making a fuss
Of me.
I don't like water much
When it touches my fur.
Can you guess what I am?
I gave you lots of clues!

Katie Minchin (9)
Oldfield Park Junior School, Bath

MOLLY

Good runner,
High jumper,
Water slurper,
Good runner,
Water dribbler,
Fishpond drinker,
Soft stroker,
Fast eater,
Good sniffer,
Snore sleeper,
Black spotter,
My dog Molly.

Stacey Jones (9)
Oldfield Park Junior School, Bath

SWEETS

When my friends are eating sweets,
Toffee, peppermint, oh what a treat,
The scent of perfume
Like my mum's
It's even better than sucking our thumbs.
Big, small, colourful too
Making colours better than you.
The crinkly paper - crinkle, crinkle
Makes the colours - sprinkle, sprinkle.
When it's time to go to bed
Sweets, sweets run through my head.

Nervana Barron (8)
St Benedict's RC Primary School, Midsomer Norton

THE HILLS OF EXMOOR

Swelling hills threatening to burst,
A blister on man's geometric landscape,
Purple pock-marks and leather brown,
Perfect coat of heather and gorse,
Broken by creeping, cat-back firs.

Clouds snatch colour away as they pass,
Leaves things mystified and silent,
Stealthy and cruel they darken the land,
Speeding away across the hills.

The coast stuck together unevenly,
As wrinkled as an ancient face,
Endless crinkly lines and creases,
With waving sea beyond these shores.

Marie-Louise Kertzman (9)
St Benedict's RC Primary School, Midsomer Norton

FOOTBALL

James to
Ashley, Ash to Millsey, Mills to
Campbell, Campbell to Rio. Boot it to
Gerrard, cross it to Nicky, back heel to
Beckham, bend it to Scholesy. Heskey
Makes a run, now take it Owen,
Dodge him, cross him, dribble
And *shoot!*
Yes! No! Yes!
What a goal!

Benedict Harrington (10)
St Benedict's RC Primary School, Midsomer Norton

WINTER

Don't be so cold-hearted,
Freezing people's lawns,
Plunging the Earth into darkness,
Numbing people's feet,
Taking the scenery away,
Covering the pavements in ice,
I'm sometimes irritated as well
But I don't go around killing people's flowers.

Laura Kor (10)
St Benedict's RC Primary School, Midsomer Norton

WHAT A GOAL?

'Owen's got the ball . . .
Passes it to Gerrard . . .
Oh no! He's been tackled . . .
But Beckham's tackled back . . .
Wow!
That was a fantastic goal!'

Catherine Singh (10)
St Benedict's RC Primary School, Midsomer Norton

WINTER

Don't be so cruel,
Stop covering my flowers,
Splatting on my roof,
Freezing up my fingers,
Crashing on my windows,
I've gone crazy too,
But I don't rant and rave about it.

Lara Cockhill (11)
St Benedict's RC Primary School, Midsomer Norton

The Tornado

I can thrash, I can spin,
I can damage anything.
I can be cone shaped, I can be round,
I can pull tree roots out of the ground.
I can be kind, I can be good,
If I could help you then maybe I would.
I can be bored, I can be mad,
I can be happy and I can be sad.
I can party for 24 hours,
I can be clever with all my powers.
I don't fear snow, I don't fear rain,
Fire and hailstone, well they're just a pain.
I can be born at the start of the day,
Then in a few hours, I'll die away.

Robert Spence (11)
St Benedict's RC Primary School, Midsomer Norton

My School

I don't like my school,
The teachers are horrible to me.
I really don't like my school,
There's children older than me.
I really, really don't like my school,
My friends are nasty to me.
I asked my mum not to go today,
But she sent me anyway.
I really don't like my school,
It's nasty to me!

Jessica Winsley & Flora Stevens (9)
St Benedict's RC Primary School, Midsomer Norton

HARBOUR BAY

Lily pads in twilight
Dancing by the moonlight
And when the morning comes
The leaking light of day returns
And all this beauty sneaks away
Until the end of this day.
When it comes back out at night
It beckons back the silver light
To shine upon the lily pad
Which once the grasps of water had.
Now nothing but a pile of leaves
Stands among the dampened reeds
In light of the silver ray
Of the moonlit Harbour Bay.

Sophie Symons (11)
St Benedict's RC Primary School, Midsomer Norton

DRAGONS

Dragons have sharp claws,
I can smell lots of smoke,
Hear crackles and roars,
It has sharp teeth,
I can feel warm breath,
It has a forked tongue,
Hot fire, yellow eyes,
Big horns,
Orange wings,
Scaly skin.

Harry Morris (8)
St Benedict's RC Primary School, Midsomer Norton

DARK FEAR

Don't be so terrifying,
Stop scaring me out of my wits,
Raising the hairs on the back of my neck
So I daren't move.
The dangerous killer at night,
The deep silence at night,
The screams and the howls of the storm,
I'm lonely in the world as well
But I don't frighten people about it.

Jennifer Liddle (11)
St Benedict's RC Primary School, Midsomer Norton

WINTER

Don't be so grouchy,
Stop ruining my flowers,
Freezing the windows rapidly,
Setting ice traps slyly,
Freezing up the ground,
I'm sometimes cross as well
But I don't rave and rant about it.

Amy Milverton (11)
St Benedict's RC Primary School, Midsomer Norton

BOOKS

Books are fun,
Books are cool,
Books are exciting
But TVs rule!

Matthew Mitchell (10)
St Benedict's RC Primary School, Midsomer Norton

THE MOON

Here I am, up in the dark night's sky,
All alone up here so high,
Beaming down on the world below,
Though I have not a finger, nor a toe,
I am so lonely, so very cold
And below me, my story is told,
Stories of a man sitting on the moon,
Maybe a real man, maybe a cartoon,
But there's only one moon, me, up high,
Cold and lonely in the dark night's sky.

So here I am in the midnight sky,
Looking down, from here so high,
Watching, watching the world go round,
Though I make no noise, nor a sound,
Shooting stars whizz by and say,
'Move aside, we want to play!'
I have no friends to talk to, no pal
For I am the moon, forever and now
I sit alone, watching up high,
Cold and lonely in the dark night's sky.

Anna Moon (11)
St Benedict's RC Primary School, Midsomer Norton

HORSES

I like horses because they are fun,
The problem is they need a lot done,
Like brushing the stable and brushing the floor
And brushing a whole lot more.
After that I go for a ride,
Hooray! Hooray! I gallop with Amy at my side.

Lucy Francis (10)
St Benedict's RC Primary School, Midsomer Norton

Autumn

A is for acorns which squirrels are collecting.
U is for underground where foxes and badgers
   make their dens to hibernate in.
T is for trees whose leaves are changing colour.
U is for umbrellas because it keeps on raining.
M is for midnight when we set our fireworks off.
N is for nuts that we roast on the bonfire.

Katherine Fox (10)
St Benedict's RC Primary School, Midsomer Norton

Snowflakes

Snowflakes are falling, it's a cold day,
Children are running in their hats and scarves today.
If I could wish something I'd wish away school every day
And play all the time and all day.
Sometimes I wonder why doesn't snow come more often,
Snow, oh snow, oh snow.

Charlotte Jones (10)
St Benedict's RC Primary School, Midsomer Norton

Skater

Flame boy
Up to the park,
Riding down the road,
Touching fences and walls,
Hands scratched and dirty feet,
Balanced normal, dodging in and out of the cars,
Up and down the vert, then 50/50.
Fell off. Smacked my chin.

Tom Gould (10)
St Benedict's RC Primary School, Midsomer Norton

WINTER

Don't be so mean,
Don't trip people up,
Stop trapping me inside.
You are freezing the ground,
Freezing my toes, icing the road.
I am stressed out as well,
But I don't take the colour out of the world.

Sam Weller (10)
St Benedict's RC Primary School, Midsomer Norton

SNOW

Cold snow, shivering snow,
Snowflakes flowing in white slippery snow.
Ice frozen in the grass in the snow.
If you go out just put these things on,
Put your gloves on, your woolly hats and coats.
Let's go and have a snowball fight in the cold shivering snow!

Bryony McDermott (7)
St Benedict's RC Primary School, Midsomer Norton

PETS

Pets are best in the world,
They are fun to play with,
They deserve a medal.
I've got a dog who protects me every day,
He never runs away,
He is the friendliest dog in St John.

Joseph Segal (8)
St Julian's Primary School, Bath

FAIRYLAND

I have been to Fairyland.
I have been to a fairy's house for tea.
I have seen cats and unicorns flying.
I have seen fairies flying in the clouds.
I have seen fairies buying biscuits and bread
And lemonade and cherryade.
I've seen fairies singing and dancing
And dusting and washing and cooking.
I've seen fairies buying new clothes.
I've seen fairies singing and dancing at night to the band.
I've seen fairies having a bath and getting into their nightgowns.
I've seen fairies washing up and having breakfast
And brushing their teeth and making their beds
And I've seen fairies flying in my garden.

Hannah Langley (8)
St Julian's Primary School, Bath

ME!

Me!
I like playing football.
Me!
I have really nice friends.
Me!
I am good at rugby.
Me!
I really, really like sports.
Me!
I am just me.

William Hughes (8)
St Julian's Primary School, Bath

FAIRIES, FAIRIES

Fairies, fairies in the air,
Fairies, fairies everywhere.
Fairies big and fairies small,
Fairies are not very tall.
Fairies don't make anything wet,
But you can't have them as a pet!

Zoe Robertson (8)
St Julian's Primary School, Bath

FAIRYLAND

I have been to Fairyland
I've heard the fairy band
I've seen pigs fly!
They oinked, 'Hi!'
I've had fairy tea
And seen a purple bee
And all because I wished on some stars
Next time I'll go to Mars!

Jade Dix (8)
St Julian's Primary School, Bath

APPEARING ANIMALS

Late at night the owl sings
the sweetest song of all living things.
And the bushbaby will jump
as high as the camel's hump.
And the squirrel leaps through the trees
as far as frogs jump through the leaves.

Oliver McGill (9)
St Julian's Primary School, Bath

GRENDEL
(Inspired by the poem 'Beowulf')

Gruesome Grendel galloped towards Herot.
He found the doors had been replaced.
Beowulf jumped
Up with a prance
Looking for his chance.
The floors creaked,
Grendel got closer and closer.
He still had an arm missing
He was hobbling a bit.
Beowulf settled down.
Grendel found them.
Beowulf hadn't got a chance.
He jumped up with a prance
When he saw him he ran.

Sam Vercoe (8)
Wiveliscombe Primary School, Taunton

GRENDEL
(Inspired by the poem 'Beowulf')

Looking down from above
At the warriors fast asleep
Down at Herot where they lay
For no one knows what he was thinking
He put out a hand
Nobody knew where he came from
He grabbed his first victim
Held it in his hand . . .

Rosie Johnson (7)
Wiveliscombe Primary School, Taunton

GRENDEL
(Inspired by the poem 'Beowulf')

The cruel bloodthirsty creature
Marching towards Herot.
Grendel's fierce eyes staring around,
His mouth dripping, tummy churning.
What was he doing?
Where was he going?
His silhouette from the only moonlight
That no one could see,
For they were asleep.
He stepped forward,
Then suddenly he tore off the door,
Right off its hinges,
Not thinking what would happen.

Sophie Prescott (7)
Wiveliscombe Primary School, Taunton

GRENDEL POEM
(Inspired by the poem 'Beowulf')

Grendel, a fierce, frightening creature
came stepping towards Herot.
His eyes reflecting on the moon, he grabbed
the door, pulling it off its frame.
Landing on the floor with a thud.
Peering around the room, his eyes as sharp as swords.
Laughing loud and high, pouncing on the nearest one.
He swallowed it whole, taking big bites
Leaving jagged teethmarks.

Freddie Kimsey (7)
Wiveliscombe Primary School, Taunton

GRENDEL
(Inspired by the poem 'Beowulf')

Gruesome Grendel as he was,
Wanted to kill, that is because,
He disliked the sounds when a feast was near,
Plus he did not like the smell of beer!
He wanted to kill, and that was that,
And he didn't even care if it made him fat!
So he went down the hill,
With a glint in his eye,
Ready to kill,
My, oh my,
He knocked on that door,
As hard as he could,
That was so nicely
Made out of wood.
It fell to the floor with an almighty crash!
And it looked like a pile of potato, mashed,
He sprang to the floor and killed two people!
Not noticing Beowulf.

Jessica Robinson (9)
Wiveliscombe Primary School, Taunton

GRENDEL
(Inspired by the poem 'Beowulf')

Over the misty moors he came,
Killer by nature and killer by name.
A fierce, foul fiend,
For one man was about to make the end,
Around the room he crept, growling!

Creeping around the hall, prowling.
He tore a warrior right in two,
The others had not a clue.
A murderer he was that night
Then Beowulf twisted his arm off with a fight.

Andrew Fudge (8)
Wiveliscombe Primary School, Taunton

GRENDEL
(Inspired by the poem 'Beowulf')

Old Grendel to Herot he came,
His usual target the same.
He knocked down the door,
He heard the warriors snore,
He was sure to be one of their bane.

Young Beowulf thought he had been beaten,
Soon one of his friends had been eaten!
But soon saw chance,
He jumped up with a prance,
It was Grendel who now had been beaten.

But Grendel soon returned,
The power of Beowulf he'd learned.
That gruesome old beast,
He had a great feast!
The warriors' fortunes had turned.

Andrew Heard (9)
Wiveliscombe Primary School, Taunton

GRENDEL
(Inspired by the poem 'Beowulf')

Grendel came out of his dark dripping cave,
Taking big steps towards Herot,
Weaving in and out of huge trees and hills,
Pushing down the big splintered door,
Looking at the warriors from above,
He picked one up,
Swallowed him whole,
Beowulf was still awake,
Grendel with eyes burning like fire,
Reached out for another one,
Picked him up,
He got up and got his arm,
Twisting it off,
Like someone wringing a soaking cloth.

Charley Chandler (8)
Wiveliscombe Primary School, Taunton

GRENDEL
(Inspired by the poem 'Beowulf')

As gruesome and grotesque Grendel looked
Over the drugged, sleeping warriors,
He laughed loud, 'Ha! Ha! Ha! Ha! Ha!' but he was
Careful not to wake the warriors.
Eagerly he pounced on the nearest warrior
And ate him whole.
Then he reached for Beowulf.

Alfie Callery (8)
Wiveliscombe Primary School, Taunton

GRENDEL
(Inspired by the poem 'Beowulf')

Towering over turrets high
Grendel roared aloud
Stepping down the echoing hallway
Slammed the door behind

Opening another creaking door
Then a trickle of dripping blood
Trickled from a leaking mouth
He grabbed for the nearest victim
Slowly swallowed him whole.

Ruby-Ann Boddington Parker (7)
Wiveliscombe Primary School, Taunton

GRENDEL
(Inspired by the poem 'Beowulf')

Grendel, that bloodthirsty terror,
In his ghastly hell-filled lair.
He strode to Herot with ravenous breath,
Burst open the splintering door.
Claws as sharp as swords.
Slashing his claws and tearing a warrior
Limb to limb.
Greedily he reached for the next,
Little reckoning for Beowulf.

Ben Toomer (8)
Wiveliscombe Primary School, Taunton

GRENDEL
(Inspired by the poem 'Beowulf')

Gruesome Grendel was ugly,
He slumped to his cave,
Treading on slugs and beetles,
Eating anyone in his way.
People were afraid of him,
They locked their doors.
He returned to Herot,
Ran into his cave and slammed the door behind him.
Suddenly! A torch flaming in his eyes
He saw some men, he scanned them.
Pouncing on the nearest, he gobbled him whole,
Looking for the last, suddenly there came a rip.
Grendel was dead!

Eleanor Finlayson (7)
Wiveliscombe Primary School, Taunton

GRENDEL
(Inspired by the poem 'Beowulf')

From a deep dark moor
There came gruesome, grumpy Grendel
And he ran to Herot
His horrible, hideous hands
Struck the studded door
And wrenched it from its hinges
He scanned the warriors
He picked a warrior and ate him whole.

James Adams (7)
Wiveliscombe Primary School, Taunton

GRENDEL
(Inspired by the poem 'Beowulf')

That horrible Grendel marched across the moor
To the hall called Herot which stood quiet and lonely
He tore off the door, splintered and old.
Ripping it in half, like a sheet of paper
That monster, Grendel, scanned the warriors
Each one fast asleep
Not knowing what was behind them
Grendel laughed
Laughed loud
His fiery eyes scorched
Reaching across inside the hall
Blocking the moonlight of midnight
He walked away with one warrior
Never to sleep or wake again.

Rachael Bashford (9)
Wiveliscombe Primary School, Taunton

GRENDEL
(Inspired by the poem 'Beowulf')

Grendel lumbering over the dark and damp swamp,
Horns glistening in the moonlight,
As he approached Herot for revenge.
Grendel's long razor-like claws,
Splintered the door to sawdust.
As he picked up a warrior,
Tore him apart and gulped him down whole.
Then little Grendel turned to Beowulf . . .

Max Norman (8)
Wiveliscombe Primary School, Taunton

GRENDEL
(Inspired by the poem 'Beowulf')

Through the mountain tops he approached
From his cold and dripping cave
Then striding down the broad flat hillside
That bloodthirsty, bone-crunching beast
Grendel he was and Grendel by name
Where was he heading?
Herot.
He had reached the ancient wooden door
Wrenching it out of its frame
The sound of the door falling flat on the ground
Echoed far over the dank, lonely moors
Which were lit only
By the paleness of the midnight moon.
He strode inside
That great vast hall.
He laughed, long and loud
The sound boomed around and around the vast hall.
His eyes were menacing, brutal
Sharp as sword
He prowled over the polished floor
Leaving a trail of muddy footprints
He stared around the hall,
Before pouncing
On the nearest warrior.
He tore him to pieces
Then gobbled them down whole
He crunched the bones with razor-sharp teeth
Before sucking up the blood with relish.

Rhianna White (9)
Wiveliscombe Primary School, Taunton

GRENDEL
(Inspired by the poem 'Beowulf')

Gruesome Grendel greedily grinding bones.
Look at his lightbulb eyes.
Stay still, sly Grendel's behind you.
He's on the loose, run, run, *aargh!*
Stay away from Herot!
Mouth-watering
Bloodthirsty
It's Grendel, fierce, frightening everything
He stinks, he's hairy, stay away from him.
Aargh!

Catherine Shackleton (8)
Wiveliscombe Primary School, Taunton

GRENDEL
(Inspired by the poem 'Beowulf')

A foul smell rose as a bloodthirsty Grendel
Climbed out of his grim lair.
His gruesome fangs as dark as the night.
His eyes fire-red.
A tail as long as a table.
He crept slowly, quietly,
Towards Herot.
Trampled over grass
And leaves.
He reached the great oak door.

Georgia McGovern (9)
Wiveliscombe Primary School, Taunton

SNOWBOARDING

Standing high up the snow-cave red mountain,
Boots clipped to the blue and green metre long board.
Everything's ready to begin, and you push off,
Whizzing past lush, green pine trees and jumping rocks.
Until there you see it, the big jump.
Closer and closer, then swoosh, you're in the cool blue air.
The ground comes nearer and you brace for a landing.
You almost lose your balance, but 'ollie' and you're back on track.
Suddenly an avalanche starts! You jump up a tree and you are safe.
As you leap down, you slip and roll into an ice cave.
Luckily you're not hurt and your board's fine.
A quick recovery is vital and you speed through the cave,
And there it is, the snow lodge and the finish.
You are greeted enthusiastically.
You win first place!

Jamie Ellis (10)
Yeo Moor Junior School, Clevedon

THE CROCODILE

The crocodile waits as calm as a bed not being used.
He waits with the dirty water dashing into his eyes
Like a red bolt of lightning.

His feet kicking into the slushy mud
As he stares at the men fishing.
Rubbing his nails into the side of the river
As he snaps out at the men
And gobbles them up whole.

Pagan Knill (10)
Yeo Moor Junior School, Clevedon

THE ORANGE DIAMOND

Swimming round in circles,
Shimmering like the sun,
He's the orange diamond,
My one!

Sparkling to blind the sun,
He's the precious one,
The florescent orange colour,
Rouged up the sun!

His gills were priceless,
You couldn't sell him at all,
He was just so invaluable,
His eyes were crystal balls!

Laura Burman (9)
Yeo Moor Junior School, Clevedon

KANGAROO

Kangaroo . . .
As it bounces
Like a bouncy ball
Bouncing from place to place
Trying to find a home.
Brown colours everywhere
Impossible to see
As it travels across the Australian plain
The plain's as hot as a cooker
Cooking all the plants
And cacti.

Sam Ford (10)
Yeo Moor Junior School, Clevedon

THE SADNESS OF THE CAT

The cat is . . .
A ball of fluff as she lies in her haven.
Like a teddy bear in an old nursery,
She's all alone in the corner.
Her eyes are as bright as street lamps
And are the only things you see
Because her fur is so dark.
As the wooden door swings to and fro,
She curls up like a ball of wool.
As she drifts off,
She looks like a ball of cotton,
With two golden buttons
That need to be sewn to a jumper.
Her skinny body moves breathlessly
As she sleeps in loneliness.

Becky Hilder (9)
Yeo Moor Junior School, Clevedon

THE HORSE

The horse is . . .
Gentle and slender
Like a four-legged stool
Standing so still
At the weight of his rider.

Galloping far, galloping wide
With someone on his back
He seems to say, 'See you soon.'
A horse
A friend, my life.

Sarah Gazzard (9)
Yeo Moor Junior School, Clevedon

BUTTERFLY

Butterfly
With coloured wings
Fluttering in the wind
Like a colourful rainbow
Spreading colour places
Colours everywhere
Fluttering past me.

Butterfly
With coloured wings
Like a coloured rubber
Erasing their coloured life
Not spreading colour places
But lying on the ground
Goodbye butterfly!

Alex Corrigan (9)
Yeo Moor Junior School, Clevedon

THE HORSE

The horse is like a train
Galloping on its tracks,
With feet as gentle as can be,
With its shadow against the ground,
And its tail cooling it down
As the wind blows past.

It is fast as wind
As it gallops along the tracks,
It is like the electrical tracks
Are giving the horse energy,
When it rushes past you
It feels like a tornado sucking you in.

Ashley Thornton (9)
Yeo Moor Junior School, Clevedon

EARTH

Earth is a place where animals are free.
Earth is home to the small bumblebee.
Earth is home to the tabby cat.
Earth is home to the flying black bat.

Earth is a place where nature sprouts.
Earth is home to the swimming trout.
Earth is home to the puny flea.
Earth is home to the big oak tree.

Earth is a place of many countries.
Earth is home to many trees.
Earth is home to the killer whale.
Earth is home to the flying quail.

Earth is a place where animals are free.
Earth is home to you and me.
Earth is home to animals herds.
Earth is home to many birds.

Andrew Ham (9)
Yeo Moor Junior School, Clevedon

THE MONKEY WHO FOUND A FRIEND

Josh, the baby monkey
Loved eating KitKat Chunkies.
He liked watching TV
Whilst drinking a cup of tea.

One day the monkey, Josh
Made himself a drink of squash,
Then he went to jump up,
Then he broke his mum's nice cup.

Josh Cope (10)
Yeo Moor Junior School, Clevedon

THE FOX

The midnight fox runs swiftly through the forest
Like a cheetah
Leaping on its prey like a tiger
Suddenly it strikes and the prey is dead

The fox is just about to pounce
Then it strikes again
On a little mouse
Like a lion on its prey

Dragging the mouse to its bush
The mouse is dead
It's like a crocodile
Taking its prey to its den.

Aaron Bray (10)
Yeo Moor Junior School, Clevedon

THE HORSE

The horse is like a white cloud
Galloping through the air
His legs so powerful
Like a bolt of lightning
He tears the grass to pieces
As he wildly returns to home

His silky mane full of sparkles
Swishes along with the breeze
But up high in the sky his father gallops with him
So gentle and so elegant.

Philippa Crossland (9)
Yeo Moor Junior School, Clevedon

THE KITTEN

The kitten's walking through the dark street
Looking for his home,
Thinks he's lost for good . . .
Wanting his home.

He wishes he could be at home,
Sleeping by the fire,
All warm and cuddled up,
He dreams of his home.

His fur is all shaggy and wet,
It used to be the opposite,
He's lonely on his own,
He wishes he was home.

His miaows are so cute and quiet,
Suddenly someone comes,
He thinks, *my owner!*
Maybe it's home.

Could it be? Yes it is,
She takes him in,
And gives him food,
I feel this is home.

She gives him a nice warm bath,
Now his skin is . . .
Warm and beautiful,
Like it used to be.

He's safe and sound now,
Sleeping by the fire, not moving at all,
Like a grey rock,
Solid, firm and safe.

Freja Lovett (9)
Yeo Moor Junior School, Clevedon

The Monkey

The monkey,
In the jungle,
Swinging from tree to tree,
Brown with a lovely grey chest,
He gets hungry,
Still swings on,
He sees a banana tree,
Desperately jumps but it's too far,
Just misses,
Hits the floor like an elephant stamping,
Fortunately he's not hurt,
Gets up,
Scrambles up the tree,
Grabs a banana,
Eats it, again grabs a banana,
Eats it, he could go on all day,
Oh no!
Sees a jaguar,
Swings quickly away,
The jaguar runs after him,
The monkey screams and screams,
Finally sees a tall tree,
Climbs up as fast as lightning,
The predator gives up and strolls off,
The monkey climbs slowly down,
The jaguar swiftly turns round,
The monkey scrambles up the tree again,
The angry jaguar gets fed up and storms off.

Sam Kacher (9)
Yeo Moor Junior School, Clevedon

THE CHEETAH

The fast mover
Of the African plain
His coat is beautiful and golden
With black spots all over
It is as black as a cave
Now the cheetah is as fast as the wind
The grass moves out of his way
He goes so fast, no one sees him
For he sees them.

The cheetah running
While in the African plain
A deer gnawing grass
The cheetah like lightning
His prey perceives the cheetah
Run does the prey
Cheetah rapidly pursuing
Leap, leap, leap
Dead!

Ashley Williams (9)
Yeo Moor Junior School, Clevedon

THE TABBY CAT

By the fireside he lies,
All curled up and asleep.
An orange glow in the light,
Like a fireball.

He slowly moves across the floor,
Slinking like a tiger.
He pounces high to catch his prey,
Alive and sleek killing machine.

Helen Newell (9)
Yeo Moor Junior School, Clevedon

THE SHARK

The shark is . . .

The lord of the sea
The shark's fin swishes through the water
Like a sharp blade
His long, pointed jaws are ready to snap
Like a digger in the wall,
His eyes like headlights ready to catch his prey

The shark's tail swishes back and forth
Like a crane swinging through the open sky
Lifting the water with its power
The shark's body reflects on the outside of the deep sea
An iron-blue monster
Dominating all - they flee!

Jessica Puddy (10)
Yeo Moor Junior School, Clevedon

PUPPY!

Cuddled, warm,
Against the fire,
Comes a little yawn,
From underneath your blanket!

I think you're so cute,
Curled up in a ball,
You keep very mute,
Yet your heartbeat's
So small!

Evey Carpenter (10)
Yeo Moor Junior School, Clevedon

THE INDIAN ELEPHANT

The Indian elephant is . . .
A big lump of grey,
A huge bag of coal,
Camouflaged in-between
The rocks,
It's the trumpet of
The jungle.

Like an old grey train,
It keeps its pace and
Never loses it.
Then it slows down for its break.
The Indian elephant
Carefully sleeps.

Like a volcano rumbling,
Slowly it awakes with
A huge trumpet that
Eases out of the leaves,
Slowly plodding to the waterhole
Where the lava shall stop!

Zara Thomas (10)
Yeo Moor Junior School, Clevedon

THE CAT

Lying by the fire,
His coat glistens in the bright glow,
An orange shade lights up the room,
As he drifts off to sleep,
The fire crackles and dies out.

Emily Ayres (9)
Yeo Moor Junior School, Clevedon

My Brother

My brother is as tall as a giant
His big brown eyes like a bear's brown coat
My brother has a bright red boat
He sails with his friends right out to sea

My brother can swim really fast
He darts through the water like a shark
My brother can run as fast as a bumblebee
He can run as fast as the wind

My brother will eat anything
From turkey to Brussels sprouts
My brother is a Boy Scout
My brother is special to me.

Jack Courtney (9)
Yeo Moor Junior School, Clevedon

Horses

The black horse is . . .
Thunder across the sky,
Galloping with a thud,
Racing like lighting in the sky,
Flashing through the trees,
Like lightning in the sky.

The white horse is . . .
Clouds floating across the grass,
So bright when the sun is out,
Just like a cloud,
When it starts to rain,
Your coat turns to grey,
Just like a cloud.

Rhianne Williams (10)
Yeo Moor Junior School, Clevedon